*Dr. Dyer,
Survive in style... Always Be Prepared!*
Alan Corson

THE FAMILY GUIDE TO
SURVIVAL

Skills that Can Save Your Life and the Lives of Your Family

ALAN CORSON

BALBOA
PRESS
A DIVISION OF HAY HOUSE

Copyright © 2013 Alan Corson.

All rights reserved. No part of this book may be used or reproduced by any means, graphic, electronic, or mechanical, including photocopying, recording, taping or by any information storage retrieval system without the written permission of the publisher except in the case of brief quotations embodied in critical articles and reviews.

Balboa Press books may be ordered through booksellers or by contacting:

Balboa Press
A Division of Hay House
1663 Liberty Drive
Bloomington, IN 47403
www.balboapress.com
1-(877) 407-4847

Because of the dynamic nature of the Internet, any web addresses or links contained in this book may have changed since publication and may no longer be valid. The views expressed in this work are solely those of the author and do not necessarily reflect the views of the publisher, and the publisher hereby disclaims any responsibility for them.

The author of this book does not dispense medical advice or prescribe the use of any technique as a form of treatment for physical, emotional, or medical problems without the advice of a physician, either directly or indirectly. The intent of the author is only to offer information of a general nature to help you in your quest for emotional and spiritual well-being. In the event you use any of the information in this book for yourself, which is your constitutional right, the author and the publisher assume no responsibility for your actions.

Any people depicted in stock imagery provided by Thinkstock are models, and such images are being used for illustrative purposes only.
Certain stock imagery © Thinkstock.

ISBN: 978-1-4525-7249-9 (sc)
ISBN: 978-1-4525-7247-5 (hc)
ISBN: 978-1-4525-7248-2 (e)

Library of Congress Control Number: 2013907195

Printed in the United States of America.

Balboa Press rev. date: 04/29/2013

This book is dedicated to my wonderful wife Gail, who has stood by me on more adventures than I'm sure she would care to remember. Never wavering, never complaining, like an oak she was, and continues to be the strength in my life that I will always cherish . . . .

Friendship honored:

Scott Anderson—The most generous individual I have ever met. I am honored to have you as my friend. May God's face shine upon you and your family.

Richard Geistwhite—A true friend who will always stand beside you even when things are going to hell around you. We were there many times . . .

Noel Wolfe—My friend. A world class adventurer. I am privileged to have spent time with you in Zimbabwe.

Rocky Duff—Former Army Ranger, Christian brother, hunting partner, no man could ask for a better friend.

Family:

Shayne and Jamie—Better daughters no father has ever had.

Tasha, Joshua and Rebekah—My grandchildren. I feel sorry for other grandparents who do not have the best grandchildren in the world!

Illustrator: Aaron Parrott, Look Outside Graphic Design, Wenatchee, Washington www.facebook.com/LookOutside

Editors: Gail Corson and Peg Plavin

ABOUT THIS BOOK

As I write this book I try to imagine anything on earth that I would want to protect more than my family. Nothing comes to mind.

While a lot of value is put on our worldly possessions, when it really comes down to it nothing is more valuable to us than our family and those we love.

There are many books today that talk about survival. Many of these books are written and oriented to military personnel and special operations soldiers who use survival skills as the very essence of what they do for a living. Other books are directed to the "hardcore survivalist" who would rather live deep in the woods or away from society predicting the end of times. That is not the intent of this book. You will not find any discussion in this book on fortified bunkers, camouflaged fighting pits, homemade explosives or other hardcore survivalist material.

This book is not intended to teach survival skills to those who already have many years of experience and training. While some of the survival skills that are contained in this book are currently used by military personnel (because these skills work), this book is designed and intended to be used by ordinary fathers and mothers, and through them to their children.

Whether we are ready or not catastrophic events do happen. At some time in your life you are likely to be in a super storm, earthquake, hurricane, tornado or manmade disaster that will challenge your ability to survive. What you have done to prepare for a disaster will play an important part in determining whether you live or die.

All too often in cases where disaster hits, only one member of the family may have some basic understanding of survival skills and other members of the family do not. What happens if the person with survival skills is injured, away on a trip or just becomes separated from the family in a disaster? What happens to the rest of the family that do not have these survival skills? What happens to the most precious things in your life?

Part of good survival training and preparation is to insure that all adults and older children in the family are equipped with these basic survival skills. Learning basic survival skills in today's society is vitally important for all adults and older children. This book is specifically designed and intended to provide these life-giving skills.

Learning survival skills can be fun for the whole family. More importantly, these skills can save your life.

I strongly encourage everyone reading this book to resist the temptation to throw a few extra cans of food in a container in the garage or make themselves a "bug out bag" tossing it into the closet, and then feeling that they are "prepared" for any emergency. I can assure you that you will not be.

It is important to learn basic survival skills and USE the items in your home emergency supply kit and in your "bug out bag" to see how they work. Get to know all of your survival equipment. Learn the techniques that will keep you and your family alive in the event of a disaster.

Get your spouse and children involved in learning the basics of making fire without matches, building shelter and living off the resources that Mother Nature provides. These survival skills will serve them for the rest of their lives.

Using your "bug out bag" equipment and your home survival equipment under controlled and non-survival conditions is not only fun but it will give you valuable experience, training, and confidence that will be priceless if you are ever confronted with a survival situation.

Developing your survival skills eventually must be practiced under realistic circumstances. Striking a match to build a fire with a wad of newspaper and dry tinder on a nice sunny afternoon will not teach you much about survival. Try that on a rainy day at dusk using a flint with tinder when you only have a few minutes before dark to build a warm fire for your camp. The more you practice the better you will get, and the more you will build your confidence.

It is important to understand that no matter how good you become with your survival skills, and no matter how much survival equipment you have with you, you must never underestimate the incredible power of Mother Nature.

Your survival training and preparation will go a long way in helping you cope with whatever may suddenly confront you.

In any survival situation you must constantly reassess your position and the events developing around you to insure that you are making the correct decisions for your survival. There is no shame in turning back when faced with a situation that could easily spin out of control and subject you to unnecessary danger.

It has been said and is very true, *"one sign of a seasoned survivalist is a person who can avoid getting themselves into a survival situation in the first place . . . ."*

INTRODUCTION

Whenever you venture away from the familiarity and security of your home, you step into circumstances that may be beyond your control. Anyone who travels, whether it is into the mountains, desert or wilderness of any kind, places themselves at some degree of risk. It just makes sense to have an understanding of the basic principles of survival and to have basic survival equipment with you.

Knowing survival skills and practicing for various situations will give you the ability to avoid panic when faced with an emergency survival situation. You will be able to clearly assess your situation, and then decide what action you need to take to survive.

Far too often people assume that everything will go as planned, and then suddenly they find themselves confronted with an emergency situation that tests their ability to stay alive. Hunters, fishermen, hikers, campers, travelers, and other recreational adventurers all deliberately move away from secure populated areas to enjoy the serenity and thrill of the outdoors.

Many people go through their daily lives not knowing that, at times, they are putting themselves at risk for a life and death survival situation. The vast majority of the time they enjoy the outing and never face any type of crisis. They do not see that the ordinary things that they do may put them into a survival event. These people assume that only those "risk takers" who travel to Africa on a dangerous game safari or those who climb mountains or hunt and hike the far wilderness of Alaska are the people who will likely find themselves faced with a survival situation. They are wrong.

The truth is that many individuals stumble into a survival situation through normal activities that they have done hundreds of times before, safely and without any adverse consequence. Survival situations are often not of your own making. You may be on an ordinary automobile trip, fishing trip, a horseback ride, on an ATV riding in the mountains, on an airplane that goes down, or a train or ship that meets disaster from a storm.

You can suddenly be faced with a life and death survival situation through mechanical failure, accident or just because Mother Nature decides to add some excitement to your life.

In these cases many individuals are at a complete loss to perform even the most basic techniques for survival. When faced with the ultimate test, they suffer and frequently they die because they did not know how to survive.

In this book you will learn that you can survive in these situations with some basic training and preparation. You will learn to make a fire to cook with and to keep yourself warm. You will learn how to find and purify water to drink. You will learn that nature offers free food for the finding and taking. You will be able to construct shelter from nature to protect and comfort you. You will learn how to find your location and navigate distances safely. In short, you will learn to survive in the wild or after a disaster in your neighborhood.

The more you learn about survival skills the more confidence you will have if you are ever suddenly put into a survival situation. Your confidence will grow with each success.

This book is intended to be used by anyone who has the desire to prepare themselves should they suddenly be faced with a survival situation. While these skills may be used by hunters, hikers and other adventurers who frequently go into the wild for recreational purposes, this book is specifically intended to address survival situations in which a person needs to utilize these skills to survive.

Warning! The techniques discussed in this book are designed for those dire situations in which your life is in danger. Some of these techniques are illegal and must not be used unless they will save your life or the life of someone in your group. Only you can make that determination.

PREPARATION

The world we live in is ripe with sudden and unexpected occurrences that force people into situations that they did not contemplate, could not foresee, and are completely unprepared to deal with.

We live in a society that has become intimately attached and dependent on the comforts of modern living. We take these comforts for granted not knowing, and for the most part not caring how these comforts make their way into our homes, offices and into our lives. A flick of a switch brings instant electricity for lighting and heating our homes. A turn of the knob brings fresh hot and cold water into our homes. A press of a lever provides all of our toiletry needs. A refrigerator and freezer hold a multitude of fresh food that we easily prepare on modern gas and electric ovens and stoves. Our modern highways give us convenient access to stores where we can buy everything we need to live our lives in comfort.

It is only on those occasions in which these modern comforts are suddenly and abruptly interrupted and we lose these life providing amenities that we suddenly realize how dependent our lives are on them. We then realize our dependency on community utilities and the immense difficulties we will face without them.

Alan Corson

We have faced disaster many times in the past.

On October 12, 2012, hurricane Sandy devastated portions of the Northeastern United States. It was the eighteenth storm and tenth hurricane of 2012. At least 253 people were killed in that storm, even with advanced warning. Hundreds of homes and businesses were destroyed or damaged. Nearly a million people were displaced—a catastrophe that crippled that area of the country.

On August 25, 2005, hurricane Katrina slammed into New Orleans flooding 80% of the city. This storm caused 1,833 deaths and devastated thousands of homes and businesses. This storm also raged and damaged areas from Florida to Texas and Mississippi costing $81 billion in damage. Over a million people were displaced which lead to an enormous human crisis seldom seen on that level in the United States.

The most deadly hurricane to strike the United States was on September 9, 1990 when a devastating hurricane slammed into Galveston, Texas. This hurricane claimed over 8,000 lives and destroyed hundreds of homes and businesses.

The eruption of Mt. St. Helens on May 18, 1980 was the deadliest volcanic eruption in recorded United States history. Even with days of advanced warning 57 people were killed. Over 185 miles of highway was damaged or destroyed.

The most devastating earthquake ever measured in the United States with a magnitude of 9.2 happened in downtown Anchorage, Alaska in 1964. The earthquake was so severe that the ground sank 11 feet in parts of the city while nearby ocean sea beds rose over 30 feet from their original position.

A powerful tsunami over 200 feet high slammed into coastal hillsides, killing many.

The west coast of the United States felt the residual effects of this enormous earthquake and it killed more than a dozen people in Oregon and California. This tsunami was so powerful that it even caused damage in Hawaii.

On December 26, 2004, a tsunami occurred in the Indian Ocean. One of the most deadly natural disasters ever recorded in modern history causing the death and injury of over 229,000 people. The earthquake that caused this tsunami was recorded at 9.1 on the Richter Scale. The catastrophe caused over 1.5 million people to be displaced.

On January 17, 1994, during the early morning hours a devastating earthquake with a magnitude of 6.7 hit Los Angeles costing more than 50 lives and injuring thousands. Large sections of major freeways collapsed including sections of the Golden State Freeway and the Santa Monica Freeway. The devastation of these major transportation routes effectively shut down transportation in large areas.

Most people agree that California, Oregon and Washington are overdue for the next major earthquake that will resemble the huge quakes that historically have hit this area before.

In the Midwestern part of the United States tornadoes and extreme hot and cold weather often cripple local utility services.

In the Northeast, severe winter storms slam wide urbanized areas. These winter storms effectively shut down ground transportation and community utilities.

The United States like the rest of the world has had its share of natural disasters in the past, and one thing we know for certain is that we will experience similar disasters in the future.

Disasters occur around the world frequently. Floods, hurricanes, tsunamis, tornadoes, super storms, and earthquakes are common in the world we live in. No area of the world is free from the unexpected wrath of Mother Nature.

Whether it is a natural disaster such as a severe snow storm, hurricane, flood, earthquake, coastal tsunami, or any other disaster that knocks out the electricity, gas, water supply, food supply, and the ability to travel on the highways, our lives change in an instant. We are confronted with an immediate survival situation in which we must depend on ourselves and not on community utilities or on the government to provide these comforts for us.

The types of disasters we face are many. The disasters can be those that we don't normally associate with the disruption of services. It can be in the form of an economic catastrophe that plunges our country's economy into ruins and shuts down the banking and retail businesses where stores are no longer being stocked with food and necessities. It may be in the form of a terrorist dirty bomb that isolates large populations from outside access.

In any disaster we know that there can soon be a break down in our society that strains the ability of law enforcement to maintain law and order. We have seen this too many times in the past.

All too often when disasters happen they are followed by roaming gangs and looters openly preying upon others. The initial disaster and the aftermath will put you and your family, and hundreds or thousands of others in a life survival crisis.

One thing is very clear. We have repeatedly seen with previous disasters that the government is unable to immediately respond to provide the essential necessities to those affected by the disaster. Sometimes it takes weeks or even months to restore the services lost in these disasters.

Many days after hurricane Katrina slammed into New Orleans we saw people in flooded conditions, standing on their roof tops begging for the government to provide them with water and food to survive.

Many of these people desperate for water gave in to the temptation and drank the contaminated flood water around them. They suffered needlessly because they simply did not know how to survive. They were not prepared.

Weeks after hurricane Sandy devastated portions of the Northeastern United Stated we saw people wandering through their destroyed neighborhoods again begging the government to furnish them with fresh water, fuel, food and temporary housing because they were suffering and at a complete loss on how to fend for themselves.

Whether a disaster affects thousands of people over a vast area or a lone adventurer who gets stranded or lost in the mountains, those who lack the basic understanding of how to provide for their own basic needs in these survival situations will at the minimum face a fearsome, despondent and miserable time, and at the worst they will face death.

Sadly, some of these people will perish after only a few days. They will die simply because they were unable to cope with the psychological shock of the disaster that took away their modern comforts that they were so completely dependent on, and because they did not have the basic knowledge, preparation, and skills to survive.

Even without manmade or natural disasters, the majority of the world lives in a mobile society and we frequently travel to locations where we may suddenly find ourselves faced with an emergency situation. A day ride into the mountains to enjoy the snow can quickly become an emergency if the vehicle breaks down, runs off a remote road or gets stuck in a snow bank miles from the main highway.

Our ability to cope with our surroundings in these events will determine whether we enjoy an unexpected adventure in which we will be able to persevere during difficult circumstances, and then later be able to share our story of survival with our family and friends or we will be faced with the misery of being completely at the mercy of the elements, not having the basic skills or preparation to survive.

Unfortunately, the individuals who lack basic survival skills will almost certainly be surrounded with life sustaining resources they could use to save their lives but their lack of knowledge of survival skills makes them blind to the life giving resources around them. Unless rescued by others, these people will likely face a slow and miserable death.

The fact is that anyone, at any time, can suddenly find themselves dependent upon their own resourcefulness to survive. Those who prepare in advance will find the going much easier than those who do not. The difference between life and death can be as simple as learning the skills to survive and preparing for any survival situation.

Mental Preparation

The first step in preparation for any survival situation is **Mental Preparation.** This cannot be stressed enough. This concept will be repeated throughout this book since it is such a critical component to survival. At this point you need to begin your mental survival preparation by accepting this motto:

I Will Never Quit. I Will Never Give Up! Never!

Understanding, believing and committing to this motto will take you a long way when confronted with a survival situation.

Fighter pilots, police officers, Special Forces soldiers, and others in high risk occupations train and prepare for the worst case scenario. They mentally go through various survival encounters and learn what to do in those situations. They mentally and physically practice these skills over and over until they are committed to memory, and to the point that these skills come as a natural reflex. The fact is that a person who is properly trained will always revert to that training when faced with a sudden traumatic situation. Those who do not have any training to rely upon will almost always panic when faced with a sudden traumatic situation. Those who train themselves are very likely to survive. Those who panic are very likely to die.

It happens to thousands of people around the world every year and it could easily happen to you too. You are suddenly and unexpectedly faced with a survival situation. What will you do? What action will you take? Will you be a survivor? Will your family survive?

The psychological realization that you are suddenly faced with a traumatic situation can be paralyzing to many. Many will never be able to overcome that paralyzing fear and their feelings of despondency, hopelessness and defeat.

These individuals feel that their situation is hopeless and as a consequence they lack the mental fortitude to survive. Their inability to control their fear will almost certainly result in their demise.

Understanding this basic psychological principal can save your life. You learn and understand that it is normal to feel angry that this life threatening situation has happened to you.

You know and understand that it is normal to be afraid and even to feel despondent because of your situation. You may even feel a great sense that it is not "fair" that you are being thrown into this situation through no fault of our own. Okay, life is not fair. The fact remains that you are in a survival situation. Like it or not. Understand these feelings and then get control of them. **I Will Never Quit. I Will Never Give Up! Never!**

It is at this point in the survival event that you must **MENTALLY** take the next important step in your survival. You need to acknowledge your feelings and then deliberately decide that you are going to move past these initial emotions to take control and implement the necessary steps for your survival. **Mentally You Choose To Live!**

You know and come to terms with the fact that you will be afraid at times throughout this ordeal but you also know that you have trained yourself for survival situations, and through this training you will be able to cope with that fear and continue with your survival efforts.

It is important that you acknowledge in the beginning of a survival situation that you face a very difficult situation. You know that survival events may test you beyond anything that you have ever done before in your life. You understand that at times you will be hungry, thirsty and may suffer out in the elements in a way that you have never experienced before. You understand that you are in a situation where injury and death may occur. By facing the survival situation you are in, you are steeling yourself and mentally preparing yourself to begin dealing with your situation to survive.

Now you need to begin taking POSITIVE steps to save your life and the lives of those who are with you, and who are depending on you.

As in any survival situation you will do some things right and you will do some things wrong. It is important to not let yourself become demoralized when things go wrong. It happens to even the most experienced survivalists. What is important is that you maintain a positive attitude. Look on the things that you did right and know that you are doing things that are helping you to survive. You look on the things that you did wrong and understand that these were mistakes that you made but you have learned from these mistakes and now you will not repeat them in the future. Remember, as long as you are still alive you are doing it right!

After you mentally decide that you are going to survive, the next step is to stop and evaluate your situation. You need to make important decisions on how you will best implement your survival.

ASSESS YOUR SITUATION

As soon as possible after any disaster you will need to assess your particular situation to begin making life saving decisions. Many factors come into play in making these decisions depending on the disaster that has happened and your particular circumstances.

The process of preparing for a disaster is not complicated or difficult. The individual circumstances of every person and every family will be different. A family living in a high rise building in a large city will have significantly different needs for preparation than a family that is living on a rural farm. There is no single "survival checklist" that you can check the boxes and then consider yourself totally prepared for any disaster.

A realistic approach needs to be made to prepare for a disaster. The first step is to acknowledge that you need to be prepared, and then begin taking the necessary steps to keep yourself and your family safe.

Disaster Preparation

The next step in preparation is to understand and assess what types of disaster you may face, what the threats are should a disaster happen, and what you will do in the event of a disaster.

By realistically assessing what your particular situation is and preparing your individual disaster plan, you will have taken a major step in your survival.

Assess where you live and work. What has been the history of disasters in that area? Do you live on the west coast of the United States or in other parts of the world where experts agree that your area is overdue for a massive earthquake? Do you live in tornado or hurricane prone states? Is your area likely to be hit by a massive flood? Do severe winter storms cripple the power grid and disrupt ground transportation in your area? Understanding the threats in your particular area will help you make a good disaster plan.

Unfortunately all too often people become apathetic about disaster events even when similar disasters have happened in the area where they live. Many people have the feeling that if a disaster hits it will effect others but not them. People who live in these disaster prone areas fail to prepare. When a disaster hits many are injured and some of them die.

Disaster Planning—At Work

A good family disaster plan has several parts. One important part is planning that you may not be at home when a disaster hits. You may not be with your family when a severe earthquake hits or catastrophic event knocks out the power and cripples transportation in your area. Your disaster plan prepares you for any such occurrence.

Your disaster plan must incorporate what you need to do if you are at work or away from home when a disaster happens.

Carefully assess your work environment and plan on how you would evacuate the building where you work. Are there different ways to evacuate your building? How will you get out if these escape routes are blocked by fire or structural damage?

Do you work on a second or third story building where a survival window ladder could save your life in the event your building is on fire and the normal escape routes are blocked?

A simple length of rappelling rope stuffed inside a bag in your office could mean the difference between living or dying if your building is on fire and a window is your only means of escape. If you work in such a building, do you have the basic skills to rappel to safety?

Can you keep a backpack in your office that contains basic survival equipment that will be easy to grab and take with you in the event of a disaster?

When you get out where will you go?

It is a good idea for your disaster plan to know where you will get the necessary items you will need to allow you to be able to survive the immediate aftermath of a disaster. You will need water (most important), food, shelter, proper clothing and footwear. You may keep some of these basic survival supplies in your vehicle at work but what if your car is parked in a parking garage and the disaster prevents you from being able to reach your vehicle?

Keep in mind that in any such disaster you will not be able to rely upon emergency rescue personnel to come and save you. Disasters by their very nature quickly incapacitate emergency responders who have a very limited ability to respond to events in mass disasters. Rescue personnel will quickly be overwhelmed by calls, their ability to drive around will be severely compromised, and they simply will not be able to respond even to the most life threatening situations.

When the power grid goes down from a disaster, motor vehicle traffic will soon begin running out of fuel and gas stations will not be able to provide fuel. Trucks and cars will slowly grind to a halt blocking major highways and secondary streets into and out of the disaster area. People will be stranded and help will not be available.

Shortly after the power grid goes out communities will no longer be able to operate facilities that provide natural gas service, running water to homes and businesses or sewage treatment services. All of these vital community services will soon stop operating.

Transportation

When a major disaster hits, thousands of people will need to be evacuated from the area. Many people will rush to get out of the city only to find the streets and highways damaged from the disaster and impassible by motor vehicles. Their stalled vehicles will only add to the clogged transportation nightmare. People will be in a panic and motor vehicle crashes will occur further obstructing the streets and highways making them virtually impassible.

Many people will be in need of immediate medical attention but the area hospitals and medical facilities will very quickly be overwhelmed by an enormous number of people who have been hurt and are in need of emergency medical attention. Hospitals and medical clinics will not be able to handle the huge number of patients that arrive for treatment. People will suffer and die because they cannot receive medical treatment.

People will need food, clean drinking water, and temporary shelter. Most will have made no preparation for these basic needs. They will be completely dependent on others to provide them with the basics they need to survive. There will quickly be a critical shortage of these supplies.

What you need to know is that there are no formal federal guidelines established to organize and facilitate this process in the event of a major disaster. The government does not have a good track record when it comes to responding to large disasters. People will be on their own for a period of time before formal assistance begins to trickle in.

The preparation you made (or did not make) will largely determine if you are going to be one of the "victims" who suffers in long lines hoping that someone will give you the very basic needs to survive or if you are prepared to deal with a disaster on your own.

A disaster plan for your work environment should also include details as to how you will be able to get out of the city to return home (or to the location you have planned to go to in the event of a disaster). Many surface streets will be severely damaged, and bridges may be washed out or damaged to the point that they are impassible. Your disaster plan should include a good map that details all streets and roads that provides several alternate routes for you to use to return home. Be sure to highlight these escape routes on your map for quick reference.

Your plan should also include the possibility that you may need to walk out to get home safely. Your map should also give details of areas away from highways and streets that you may need to travel to get home. Check the map closely for rivers, lakes or other obstacles that you may need to cross to make your way home. Make a plan on how you will circumvent these obstacles to get home. Make several alternate routes as well.

Since in many disasters the highways and roads will be impassible by motor vehicles, you need to consider alternate means of transportation. Do you have access to a bicycle? Bicycles are an excellent means of travel after a disaster hits. People all over the world use bicycles in all types of weather and on all types of paths, trails and roads. Bicycles are inexpensive, very mobile, do not require fuel (other than calories operating them), and they allow you to travel a significant distance much faster than walking. Bicycles can be used on trails and off roads where motor vehicles cannot travel. There are several fold-up style bicycles on the market that would be very useful after a disaster. Small motorcycles also offer an excellent means of transportation in the event of a disaster. These very fuel efficient motor bikes can be used both on the street and off road when necessary. A gallon of fuel will take you a long distance on these vehicles.

Check the areas on your escape route to see what water sources are available to you in an emergency. Look for rivers, lakes, streams, ponds, fountains, and other sources of water. Your backpack should have the basic means to disinfect water so you are able to have water to drink on your trek home. Your disaster plan makes a realistic estimate as to how long it may take you to get home using various routes, both by vehicle and on foot.

Your disaster plan should include how you will obtain food, although this is not a critical element in the first day or so. If your plan to return home will take you several days you should plan on how you will obtain food to eat. Can you carry enough food in your office backpack for a few days? Does your route home pass near any farms, gardens or other places where you may be able to get food? What will you do for shelter on your way home?

Do not count on stores to be stocked with food, water and other survival items after a disaster. In a matter of hours the store shelves will be stripped completely bare. You will not be able to find food, water or other needed supplies in any store.

Disaster Planning—At Home

The sad part of discussing being prepared for a disaster is that many people do not believe that a disaster will ever happen, at least not to them. Just look around to what has happened during just the past 10 years. History indicates otherwise.

Your home disaster plan should include a realistic assessment of what disaster threats you and your family may face at home, and how you will deal with these events.

We know that disasters can happen quickly and often without any warning. Learning the types of disaster that may occur in your area will help you make an effective plan to deal with those disasters. When you prepare for the common problems that you will face in a disaster you effectively prepare for those uncommon problems that may also occur.

Your home disaster plan needs to begin with a realistic understanding of where you live and the area around you. What are the natural hazards that you may face at home after a disaster?

Every home should have "home survival" supplies that are not part of the home's normal everyday food supplies.

Take an inventory of all of the supplies that you will need in the event of a disaster. You know that you will need food, water, shelter and clothing to keep warm and the ability to cook and have clean drinking water

The most frequently asked question is "what foods do I store for my emergency supply?"

Every family needs to assess their own particular needs and you certainly want to store foods that you like instead of what will just last the longest.

Sometimes people get caught up in the "survival food" hype and forget that food is food. The only difference is that you generally cannot store ordinary grocery food for 5-10 years. That is not a problem if you make a plan and simply rotate your survival food supply into your normal food that you eat, and replenish the survival supply with fresh provisions periodically.

It will not be a problem for you to store ordinary grocery food items that you normally purchase to last for 2-3 weeks after a disaster. A catastrophic disaster will require you to have provisions that will last for several months or longer. Calculate the meals necessary for each person in your family for that length of time. It is always best to plan on extra food that you may need rather than to run out. This food should be set aside from the food that you ordinarily use so that it always will be available if a disaster strikes.

Be sure that your system of rotation includes consuming the emergency supply before their expiration dates and then replenishing them with fresh provisions. Also rotate all canned goods at least every year even if they do not have an expiration date since these foods can lose their taste over time.

Here is a basic list of things that you may want to add to your home emergency supplies for long term survival. The amount of these items is dependent on just how long you want to be able to eat during the aftermath of a severe disaster.

The following foods if stored properly can last for at least 10 years.

Wheat is an essential for your long term survival food. Wheat can last indefinitely with proper storage. Wheat can be used for baking to make many foods. It also can be sprouted to give you fresh tender greens for your diet. You can use wheat as seed to grow additional food. These are the easiest to store for shelf life, nutrition and calorie sustenance. White rice will keep for many years but brown rice will only keep 6 months to 1 year.

1. Soft White Wheat

2. Hard Red Wheat

3. Durum Wheat

4. Buckwheat

5. Corn

6. Oats

7. Barley

8. White Rice

9. Brown Rice

Sugar:

1. Sugar—either brown sugar or white sugar—storage 10 years or more

2. Raw Honey—use as a sweetener and to give energy. It has an indefinite shelf life.

3. Maple Syrup

Grains:

1. Dry Corn

2. Millet

Soft Grains—will store about 5-6 years vacuum packed.

1. Oats
2. Barley
3. Rye

Flour:

1. White Flour
2. Whole Wheat Flour
3. Cornmeal

Beans: An excellent source of protein and can store for about 10-15 years:

1. Garbanzo Beans
2. Pinto Beans
3. Kidney Beans
4. Lima Beans
5. Black-eyed Beans
6. Lentil Beans
7. Soybeans

Canned goods to store—rotate yearly

1. Canned meats
2. Canned vegetables
3. Canned Fruits

1. Peanut Butter
2. Powdered Milk—(Nonfat dry milk keeps longer that dried whole milk)
3. Coffee & Tea

Cooking Oils:

1. Vegetable Oil
2. Coconut Oil—good in storage for about 2 years or so
3. Olive oil
4. Safflower oil

Salt—this is essential for your diet and health. It also can be used to preserve food. It has an indefinite shelf life.

Essential Items to have—home emergency supply:

1. Wooden matches, water proof matches, Butane lighters, fluid Zippo type lighters, fire steel and magnesium bar fire starters

2. Knife and hatchet

3. First Aid kit

4. Toilet paper & paper towels

5. All medicines and prescriptions

6. Camping stoves and extra fuel

7. Tent large enough for you and your family

8. Flashlights and extra batteries

9. Shovel

10. Small rope, twine or cord

Here is a list for those interested in Food Storage for one adult for a year:

* Wheat—variety of types / 150 pounds

* Cornmeal—50 pounds

* Powdered Instant pancake mix—50 pounds

- Beans—variety types—100 pounds
- Grains (corn, oats, buckwheat, etc) 50 pounds
- Canned or dried meats—75 pounds
- Canned fruits—50 pounds
- Canned vegetables 75 pounds
- White or Brown Rice—75/50 pounds
- Nonfat dry milk—50 pounds
- Peanut Butter—25 pounds (2 year shelf life)
- Raw Honey—30 pounds
- Sugar—30 pounds
- Powdered eggs—30 pounds
- Pasta—50 pounds
- Cooking oils—15 pounds
- Salt—15 pounds
- Dry yeast—2 pounds
- Baking Powder—3 pounds
- Variety of spices, seasoning, vitamins

You would need a good hand grain grinder to grind the grains into flour.

To properly store your emergency food supply, try to keep the provisions well below 70 degrees (F). The best temperature for non-frozen foods is between 33-40 degrees Fahrenheit. Shelf life will decrease as the temperatures increase.

Store food in sturdy containers that will keep rodents and insects out. Vacuum packing food helps extend shelf life. Keep the containers in a dark dry area.

If you are a family that has camping equipment, you already have many of the necessary items you will need to cook your food and disinfect your water when the power grid goes down. Be sure that these items are gathered and stored in a convenient location. You don't want to be rummaging around for hours trying to gather your equipment in the dark after a disaster.

It is best to store your home survival equipment in a large container such as a 30 gallon plastic garbage bin that has a snap on lid. This keeps the equipment in one area and offers some protection from damage. This container can also be used to collect and store water in an emergency.

If you have camping stoves be sure that you have several extra containers of fuel such as propane or isobutene. It is always better to have more fuel than you expect to use than to run out and not be able to acquire any more after a disaster. A second means to cook your food and disinfect your drinking water is also important.

If you use propane for your BBQ, keep an extra tank in reserve to rotate when the first tank becomes empty. That way you will always have at least one full tank on hand. If you BBQ with charcoal briquettes keep an extra bag that you can rotate in the same manner. Be sure to keep an ample supply of lighter fluid on hand too.

History has shown that people who are able to scrounge in a disaster to get things they need are the people who have a high survival rate. Those who rely on others to provide them with their necessities are in for a very bad time after a disaster hits.

Home Assessment

When you assess your home and location, consider what weaknesses your home or location may have. Do you live on a hillside that may be severely affected in an earthquake or large mud slide? Is your home located in an area that is likely to flood? Do you live in a high crime neighborhood where a disaster could trigger roaming criminal gang activity that would threaten you and your family? Does anyone in your family have a medical condition that would require special treatment? Do you have children who will need to have special food and supplies? Do you live near a chemical plant, dam or power plant that could put you in danger in the event of a disaster?

These and many other questions should be carefully considered when making your home survival plan.

When these issues are identified, make a plan on what to do in the event you are faced with any of these problems. Your careful assessment may mean that if a disaster happens you will need to leave your home and travel to a place of safety. Be sure to identify where you and your family will travel to if you need to leave your home after a disaster.

Deciding To Leave

The fact remains that in many high density cities it will be very difficult to survive after a major disaster. It is hard to imagine the calamity that results when a major disaster happens.

When simple things like running water, sanitation and garbage suddenly stop, they become a huge problem. When the streets become the open source for human sewage, and raw garbage piles up on the streets, it does not take long for disease to become a major problem. Pollution from the disruption of these services will quickly spread, adding to the death toll. We have seen many occasions in which even the brief disruption of these critical services cause huge problems in cities.

Criminal Activity

There is a certain predisposition in some individuals which takes very little to cause them to act out violently or without rational thought. We frequently see this in "mob" actions where people suddenly stampede at various events for no reason other than getting caught up in the emotion of the situation. We see violent riots break out simply because a favorite team either won or lost a game.

These senseless riots quickly spill over into the community where arson fires are set, property of innocent people is destroyed and innocent lives are placed in danger. Bystanders who just happen to be in the way are often savagely beaten simply because these rioters are out of control, and they know that they can get away with it. Large scale vandalism and looting soon follows.

Keep in mind that these violent riots are not happening because people are starving or have been without clean water to drink. They are happening because of a predisposition for violence. There is a "feeding frenzy" mentality from this violence when it becomes apparent to those rioting that they can commit these crimes and the police will not be able to stop them.

When social order collapses after a disaster, criminals who are already preying on society will have free rein to terrorize cities and law enforcement will be all but helpless to prevent it. When this occurs criminals will take over large areas of the city and any travel in those areas of the city will be especially dangerous.

Some will say this will never happen. Well, it does not take much imagination to envision a situation after a disaster in which these same individuals would, either through panic or criminal intent, exploit the disaster situation for personal gain. The history of disasters offers a clear indication of what we can expect in the future.

Consider for a moment a disaster where people begin to run out of water. They have no electricity. They have no food to eat. They are suffering from the elements without proper shelter. I can assure you that when this happens you can expect many individuals will join the ranks of those who are willing to take by force whatever they want. These individuals will do anything including murder to get the items they need to survive. Many of these individuals will gang up with others and will pose a formidable armed force to contend with. The aftermath of disasters have historically produced a dramatic increase in murder, rape, robbery and other violent crimes.

After a major disaster, a large city with high density population may be one of the most dangerous places to live or try to survive.

The fact remains that you will need to carefully assess your situation and decide if you and your family can survive in a high density city under post catastrophe conditions. For many, the collapse of a city's infrastructure will mean that they will no longer be able to survive in that city. They must leave to survive. If this is the case for you and your family, plan accordingly.

For those living in small cities or rural communities we have historically witnessed a different response to disaster.

In small towns and communities people know each other, they work together, and they socialize together at various events. They are friends and are much more willing to offer to help others in a time of need. Small towns and communities often ban together so that everyone gets the help they need. People share and are willing to do without because their neighbor is also doing without.

WHAT NEEDS TO BE DONE?

After any disaster whether it is a weather event, being lost in the mountains or after a plane crash, you need to first assess whether you are in any immediate danger or risk for further injury. It is important that you make this decision rationally and not through panic.

Whatever has happened to you it will have been a traumatic event if you find yourself in a survival situation. Make a concentrated effort to calm down and make a clear decision when assessing your situation. These initial decisions are critical in your survival. If you are in an immediate life threatening situation it is critical that your decision be correct. That decision may dictate whether or not you survive.

This initial assessment can be made in short order. The decision on whether you need to immediately move from your current location to an area of safety can be made. Proper assessment of your situation will give you the ability to decide what action you need to take to protect yourself and those who are with you.

Next, determine if you or anyone in your group is in need of medical attention. Take action to treat any injuries as soon as possible after you are sure that you are no longer in immediate danger.

There are several things that will help you assess your situation after you have reached a location of safety. With these assessments you will be able to decide what you need to do next:

* Assess your current surroundings/environment.

* What obstacles are you facing in this environment?

* Are you in a hot environment where water is an urgent need?

* Are you in a cold environment where immediate shelter is the most urgent need?

* Make a careful inspection of all of the equipment that you can use for survival. Is there anything else around you that you can collect and add to your kit for your immediate or extended survival?

* Assess your physical condition and any injuries that you may have that may limit your ability to carry out survival activities. Assess the physical condition of each member of your group. Get an understanding of their abilities and limitations.

* Use all of your senses to assess your situation. Look all around you both close up and as far as you can see. Are you able to see anything that will aid in your survival? Are you able to see or hear anything in the distance that indicates human activity?

* Are you near a sizeable river? Following rivers downstream, if possible, will frequently lead to civilization.

* Are you able to safely climb a tree to better see your surroundings? Can you move to a higher point for a better look to assess your situation?

* Do you know where you are? If so, this will help you make good decisions on what you need to do and where you need to go.

* Assess how you will accomplish this task and what you will need to do to survive in the process.

* Make a survival plan before you begin your journey.

* If you are in a group discuss this plan with everyone.

* Do you know a clear way to get out?

* Can you estimate the distances to get outside help?

* Will you be able to give your location to those who may be able to rescue you?

* Are you in a situation where you will need to rescue yourself?

* If you are then accept that fact, and begin focusing all of your attention and energy in accomplishing your own rescue.

* Are you in a location (or can you get to a location) where you can put out visual aids that will help rescuers find you?

The skills that you learn in this survival book will go a long way in preparing you to use the home survival supplies and the equipment that you have in your bug-out-bag to improvise and to solve problems you encounter along the way. You will find extreme satisfaction in solving simple problems that help you with your survival goals.

You should also understand and actually plan that you will have some survival equipment with you but that equipment may get lost or damaged beyond repair. You may be in a survival situation longer than expected and you may use up your stock of fuel, food and other survival provisions.

Using your survival skills you must be able to improvise in any survival situation to accomplish your survival tasks. Your ability to improvise in these situations may mean the difference of continuing your survival with some degree of comfort or continuing your survival in absolute misery . . . or not surviving at all. Be innovative.

Improvise To Stay Alive

You should be constantly thinking about what you can do to improvise and improve your current situation. You may surprise yourself at how resourceful you can be when it really counts. If you are in a group survival situation, encourage others to be actively thinking about what can be done to help with the survival situation. The more minds you have working to solve the problems the better.

Do Not Panic

This is probably a good time to mention something about panic. Panic is *"a sudden sensation of fear which is so strong as to dominate or prevent reason and logical thinking, replacing it with an overwhelming feeling of anxiety."* Panic may occur in a single person or in a group of individuals (mass panic).

Panic is something that must be understood and recognized but it cannot be tolerated in a survival situation. It offers no meaningful solution to any circumstance and it has the contagious effect of spreading like wildfire to others. People who are overcome by fear cannot make rational decisions even to save their own life. They react to their fear, feelings and to their imagination, and not to the actual situation they are in. This panic can be debilitating to the point of complete incapacitation.

A person who has mentally prepared for a survival situation may have "fear" but they are not likely to have "panic" fear that is so strong that it prevents them from gaining control of themselves and then making good decisions to enhance their survival. As mentioned earlier, those who have no such training are much more likely to panic on any given survival situation, and these individuals must be dealt with immediately and before that panic spreads to others.

One sure way of dealing with a panicked individual is to give that person clear, simple and concise instructions to follow and simple physical tasks to do. Generally a person who is in a panic state will grasp onto any such instructions and as they busy themselves with these simple physical tasks they begin to get their mind occupied on positive matters and are then able to release their uncontrolled fear.

What you are actually accomplishing is that you are replacing the sensation of "fear" which is so strong and dominating with simple physical tasks that allow the person to focus their mind on the task at hand and not concentrate on the fear they have. You are replacing their anxiety with positive actions.

It is important in group survival situations for a person who has survival training to take charge and give others clear instructions on what needs to be done to implement their survival. Your calm demeanor will have a direct impact on others and will motivate them to engage in positive tasks that will aid in their survival. Generally, those who do not have any such training will readily follow that lead and comply with the person in charge.

Work Together

If you are with your family or in a group survival situation it is important to delegate responsibilities so that every person not only shares the work that needs to be done but they also feel connected and actively involved in their own survival. If you are the leader you have the responsibility that your decisions will affect everyone in the group. Make your decisions wisely. It is also a good idea to carefully listen to the ideas of others and evaluate that information before deciding on what course of action needs to be taken.

If you are away from home when a disaster strikes, careful planning is essential to your survival.

Things to do after a disaster:

When in a safe area, assess all of the survival equipment that you have available to you at that time. If you are stranded in the mountains, that special hunting knife or the Zippo lighter that you left at home is of no value to you now.

Don't waste time agonizing on what could have been. Make a realistic evaluation of your equipment, the number of people with you and the particular situation you are in.

Assess individual needs and limitations. You may be in good physical condition but others with you may be injured or of an age or have health conditions that prevents them from hiking miles through rugged terrain to reach safety. If you are in a group, you are only as strong as the weakest member of that group. If you intend to move, remember that you can only move as fast as the slowest member of the group. Make this information part of your survival plan.

After you reach a location of safety you can then continue to assess your situation and decide if you or your group needs to move to a location that affords better opportunities for discovery and rescue. Can you and all members with you make that journey?

Decide on the location that will offer you the best chance of survival and the survival of those with you.

BUG-OUT-BAG

This is a list of items everyone should have in a backpack—Bug-Out-Bag. Keep this backpack in your vehicle and take it wherever you go in case of an emergency. It will not help you if you don't have it with you! This kit can save your life!

You will want to pare down the essential items for survival kits that you keep in a backpack at work to meet those specific needs. This list will give you a good idea of the items you need to have.

People frequently ask 'what are the most important things to have in a bug-out-bag.'

In cases where you are traveling by commercial airline you will not be able to carry certain items through airport security. You need to pare down your survival gear to carry those absolutely necessary items as listed in "Priority One" below. You won't be able to get through the airport security with lighters, matches or a knife. Instead carry magnesium fire starters and fire steel. They will pass through airport security. You will need to improvise to find a knife and other tools if a survival situation develops.

It is important to prioritize your survival kit. You begin with the absolute necessities that will be used to save your life. When an emergency hits you will want each of these items to be immediately accessible to you so you can grab them and go. It would be nice to have that favorite comfortable camping chair but that is not something that is essential to your survival.

Priority One: This survival gear consists of the following items you will immediately need to have access to for your survival. All of this should fit nicely in a small pack:

* Quality backpack to carry all survival gear

* Fire starters & tinder (lighters, magnesium bar, fire steel, waterproof matches)

* Water disinfection (Life Straw, iodine, chemical tablets).

* Whistle

* Water bottle/canteen

* Knife

* Navigation—compass & maps

* Mess kit—one small stainless steel pot with tight fitting lid and bail handle.

* Medical kit

* Outdoor clothing/boots

* Crank flashlight

* 10'x10' piece of painter's plastic

- Cordage (small cord, twine, or small rope—50')

- Snare Wire (22 gauge—100' roll)

- Small folding shovel or trowel (digging tool)

Priority Two: The second priority of survival gear adds the following things that you would need to stay safe on a daily basis:

- Appropriate outdoor clothing

- Emergency food—(MRE's, hiker packaged food)

- Backpack stove & fuel (alcohol/methane, butane, gas)

- Small tarp for shelter

- Personal hygiene items

- Small hatchet, large fixed blade knife

- GPS (hand tracking/location device)

- Plastic garbage size bags

- Pair of pruning clippers

Priority Three: The third priority of survival gear consists of all of the other items that you will need to sustain you for a longer period of time. The amount and type of gear will depend on the environment you are in.

Each of these items will be discussed in detail later in this book. On the following pages I have rated each of these items using a five star system on how important they are to have with you in your bug-out-bag. The ratings for these items are based upon all weather and all survival conditions.

* Fire starters—At least two in your kit.

* Butane (disposable) Lighters

* Fire Steel fire starter   (airport safe)

* Magnesium Fire Starter Bar   (airport safe)

* Zippo style lighter & fuel

* Wooden matches (strike anywhere type)

* Paper matches

Tinder: Used to first start your fire

* Cotton balls w/ Vaseline—(excellent)

* Dryer Lint—w/ candle wax

* Commercial stick fire starter bars

* Candles (not really tinder but excellent to start fires)

* Cedar Sticks (cut shavings to start fire)

* Cedar shavings with candle wax

* Char Cloth (processed cotton material that will catch a spark)

* Fat wood (pine wood with sap)

* Shelter: one 6'x8' tarp (Very Important)

* Knife—at least one good folding knife and one good fix blade knife with sheath

* Water: (very important) Drinking straw—(water disinfection filter straw—20 gallons)

* Water disinfection tablets

    * Iodine—water disinfection

    * Bleach—unscented

    * Water disinfection bottle (purifies water in bottle then drink)

    * Plastic canteen or plastic water bottle to collect, hold and purify your water

* Alcohol Stove—(you need one 12 oz. bottle of "Heet"—Gas line anti-freeze for fuel)

** I will discuss all types of survival stoves later in this book.

* Mess Kit (metal pan, pot with lid, cup)

* Twine: waxed twine, roll small nylon cord, para-cord, light rope etc.

* Snare wire (22 gauge galvanized wire—snares, shelter, etc)

* First Aid Kit: bandages, anti-septic, gauze, tape, etc.

* Crank Flashlight (2)

* Fishing kit: line, hooks, weights, lures—maybe a small collapsible rod/reel

* Metal Cup (coffee, soup, etc.)

* Stocking hat, or balaclava, gloves and extra pair of wool socks

* Emergency blanket

* Folding saw—(Used to cut branches to build shelter/fire)

* Water Proof clothes

* Sewing kit

* Bar soap and plastic container

* Small towel—wash cloth

* Small survival hand chain saw

* Small knife sharpener

* Pair scissors

* Back-up Compass

* Small hatchet (solid metal handle is best with sheath)

* Small Leatherman's tool

* Black plastic garbage bags

* Compact mirror (signaling, personal use, etc)

* Folding shovel or trowel

Food Items

* Powdered milk, packaged soups, nuts, trail food mix, dried food

* Book on survival

* Aluminum Foil (cooking)

* Small amount of Toilet Paper/Paper towels

* Anti-bacterial Wipes (these are also good fire starters)

* Individual packaged: Plastic Spoon, Fork, & Knife

* P38 Can Opener (for key chain)

* Small pump container of Deet—mosquito repellant

* Emergency solar/crank radio—(AM/FM and all Emergency Stations)

* Small firearm and ammo (break down Ruger .22 rifle or other such firearm)

* Boots (I tie a good used pair of boots on my bug out bag)

* Sheet of painter's plastic 10'x10'

* 3-4 feet of ¼" surgical tubing (solar still and drinking straw)

* Small magnifying glass

* Small Bible (this may be the last thing to go into your bag . . . but the first to come out in an emergency . . .)

Organize. It is best to organize the contents of your Bug-Out-Bag. For example, keep all elements to start fires in a plastic bag in one area. Keep all items needed to purify water in another area. Put all of your personal hygiene items in another. Put your flashlight in an outside pocket of the backpack because you are sure to need easy access to a flashlight if it is dark outside when an emergency hits (you don't want to spend time rummaging through your bag to find a flashlight when an emergency happens at night).

The best way to know what you will need in your Bug-Out-Bag is to USE IT! Make it fun to go out and use the various items in your bug out bag. See if you can start a fire without matches, purify water to drink and cook a meal. Make a shelter and see how it works. The more familiar you are with the contents of your Bug-Out-Bag the more confidence you will have if you ever face an emergency and need to use this kit to save your life.

You do not have to travel to the mountains or desert to frequently practice these basic skills. Make it fun. Have family members start the afternoon charcoal BBQ with fire steel or a magnesium bar and tinder (no cheating by using lighter fluid!). Start the evening outdoor fire pit using these tools. See if all members of the family can accomplish this. With a bit of practice they all will soon become very proficient at this life saving skill.

Routinely go through your Bug-Out-Bag (at least every 6 months to a year) and replenish those items that become outdated (food, medicine, water disinfection elements). Always keep your bug-out-bag's contents fresh and ready to go if needed.

Important: This Bug-Out-Bag can save your life and the lives of your family in times of an emergency. When putting your bag together it is very important to use quality items. The last thing you want is to have cheap equipment in your bug-out-bag that break or fails just when you need them the most!

The survival items below are rated using a five star system. One star is nice but not critical. Five stars is something that you absolutely want to have with you in any survival situation.

First, let's start with the "Bug-Out-Bag. * * * * *

This will be the container that you use to carry all of your survival gear so it needs to be a quality backpack. This pack may be subjected to some heavy use so it needs to be rugged and durable. Do not buy a cheap backpack and then become disappointed when it falls apart with a bit of rugged use.

Check the construction of the pack to see that it is well sewn. The zippers should be heavy duty and well stitched into the pack. The pack should have several separate zip-up compartments which allow you to segregate your gear accordingly. You don't want a pack with a single compartment which makes you dig to the bottom whenever you need something. The shoulder straps should be wide and padded, and not something that will dig into your shoulders when walking. These straps need to be adjustable so you can make them fit your body depending on what you are wearing. Side webbing compartments on the outside of your pack make it convenient to carry items frequently used. (flashlights, water bottles)

I like the size and design of the U.S. military backpack. They are rugged proven packs but anything similar that is quality made will do. You will probably pay top dollar for a backpack at an outdoor specialty sports store but you can find many quality backpacks at reasonable prices at other convenience stores or on the Internet.

1. Fire starters * * * * *

Having the ability to make fire in a survival situation is vital to your survival. I carry three different fire starters in my kit. They take up very little room and are well worth having.

My personal favorites are the Zippo fluid lighter, butane lighters, and the Fire Steel Match Blaster. All are easy to use. In the event you are with others in a group survival situation and you need to leave them to get help, you can always give them one of your fire starter's while you are gone. Steel Metal Strikers and Magnesium bars go through airport security.

Fire Steel Metal Striker * * * * *   (Ferrocerium steel rod)

Magnesium Bar * * * * *   (Magnesium-alloy rod)

Zippo style lighter * * * * *

Butane (disposable) lighter * * * * *

Wooden matches (strike anywhere type) * * * *

Paper matches * *

2. Tinder: Used to first start your fire

Cotton balls w/ Vaseline * * * * * (excellent—my personal favorite)

    Fire starter with cotton balls and Vaseline are easy to make and will burn even in wet conditions. To make them gather a handful of cotton balls and then generously rub Vaseline onto them mixing in the Vaseline well.
    The cotton balls should be thoroughly coated with the Vaseline but not to the point that they are a sticky ball of goo. Put the finished cotton balls with Vaseline into a heavy plastic bag and stuff them into your bug-out-bag. To start a fire just retrieve a cotton ball and set it on fire with your lighter, steel

metal striker, flint or anything else that makes a spark. The cotton ball will quickly catch a spark and start to burn. It will burn for several minutes depending on the size of the cotton ball and the amount of Vaseline on it. Just add other dry tinder and you will soon have a nice crackling hot fire.

Dryer Lint—w/ candle wax * * * *

This is another easy way to make a fire starter that works exceptionally well. All you need is the lint from your home dryer and a candle. Put some newspaper down as a protective base, and then spread out the lint. Take a candle and slowly drip candle wax all over the lint mixing it in thoroughly. When the lint is lightly coated with wax put it into a heavy plastic bag (making it water tight) and stuff into your pack. To use, just pull out a pinch of lint and set it afire with any type of spark or flame. The lint will burn long enough for you to add additional dry tinder to start your fire.

Char Cloth. * * * *

Char cloth will easily catch a spark and will glow embers long enough for you to add dry tinder to start your fire. This is easy to make and will be discussed later in the book.

Fat Wood * * * * *

This is simply pine wood heavily saturated in pitch or resin. It can be found in some pine tree stumps. In any survival situation fat wood will easily start your fire. It can be used as both a tinder and kindling.

Commercial stick fire starter bars * * * * * (very good but expensive).

Candles (even birthday candles are good). * * * * *

   Candles are not actually tinder but are excellent to start your small pile of tinder burning. When the tinder is burning, remove the candle and add additional fuel. Keep the candle for later use. One candle will make many fires. I carry a candle stub and three Votive candles in my bug-out-bag.

Cedar Sticks (shavings to start fire). * * * * *

   Carry several small 4"-5" x 1" kiln dried cedar sticks in your pack (wrapped in a plastic bag to keep them dry). Use your knife to shave these sticks putting the dry shaving into a small pile to help start your fire.

Cedar shavings with candle wax (same as above).

3. Shelter: * * * * * One 6' x 8' tarp (This is an essential piece of your survival gear).

4. Knife: * * * * * Probably the most important tool in your survival kit. You need at least one good folding knife, and one good fixed blade knife with sheath.

   Your large fixed blade knife should have a 6"-8" length robust blade made of high carbon steel or other quality steel with a good handle. This knife needs to be built for rugged outback use and capable of splitting medium size sticks and other similar work.

   Your folding knife should also be a high quality lock-blade knife. The blade length should be around 4 inches in length. The folding knife performs all of your smaller work where a large blade would be too cumbersome to use.

I prefer a non-serrated blade since these blades are much easier to sharpen.

Knife Sharpener: * * * *

As part of your kit you will need a good lightweight plastic knife sharpener. These sharpeners have two sets of ceramic bars that sharpen the blade.

You could also use a small sharpening stone that is fine grade on one side and coarse on the other. Always keep your knives sharp in the field. A sharp knife makes the work much easier and safer to do. A very dull knife blade is harder to sharpen.

5. Water: This is the most important element to have in a survival situation. You cannot go very long without it.

"Life Straw". * * * * *   (excellent)

Water disinfection tablets * * * * *   (discussed later)

Iodine—water disinfection * * * * *   (discussed later)

Bleach—unscented * * * *   (discussed later)

Water disinfection bottle * * * * * (purifies water in bottle then drink)

Plastic canteen or plastic water bottle * * * * *

6. Alcohol Stove—* * * * * (you need one 12 oz. bottle of "Heet"—Gas line anti-freeze or other appropriate fuel)

** I will discuss all types of backpacking and survival stoves later.

7. Mess Kit (metal pan, pot with lid & cup, etc.) * * * * *

8. Twine: waxed twine, roll small nylon cord, para-cord, light rope etc. * * * * *

9. Snare Wire—22 gauge wire (snares, shelter, etc.). * * * * *

10. First Aid Kit: bandages, anti-septic, gauze, tape, etc. * * * * *

11. Crank Flashlight (2). * * * * *

These battery-free flashlights are excellent for survival use. A minute of cranking on these lights will give you 30 minutes or so of good light. The bulbs will last for hundreds of hours. This is an essential piece of equipment for your survival kit.

12. Fishing kit. * * * * (line, hooks, weights, lures—small collapsible rod/reel, & spool of carpet thread) This kit can be a life saver if you are near waters that hold fish. It is much easier to catch fish with commercial fishing hooks (which easily go into your pack) rather than trying to fashion a fishing hook in the wild. Stuff some quality hooks and fishing supplies in your kit.

13. Metal Cup (coffee, soup, water) * * * * *

14. Stocking hat, or balaclava, gloves and pair of wool socks * * * *

15. Emergency blanket * * * *

16. Folding saw—(Used to cut branches to build shelter/fire) * * *

17. Water Proof clothes. * * *

18. Sewing kit * *

19. Bar soap and plastic container * * * * *

20. Small towel—wash cloth * * *

21. Small survival hand chain saw * * *

22. Pair scissors * *

23. Small Leatherman's tool * * * *

24. Black plastic garbage bags * * * * * (at least 2—catch water, sit on, stay dry, carry items)

25. Compact mirror (signaling, personal use, etc) * *

26. Food Items: * * *

Powdered milk, packaged soups, nuts, trail food mix, MRE's, other lightweight non-perishables that you can carry in your bug-out-bag.

27. Book on survival * * * * *

28. Aluminum Foil—(cooking, etc) *

29. Small amount of Toilet Paper/Paper towels * *

30. Anti-bacterial Wipes (these are also good fire starters) * * *

31. Individual packaged: Plastic Spoon, Fork, & Knife * * *

32. P38 Can Opener (for key chain) * *

33. Small pump container of Deet—mosquito repellant *

34. Emergency solar/crank radio—* * * (AM/FM and all Emergency Stations) no batteries required.

35. Small firearm, ammo & cleaning kit * * * (break down Ruger .22 rifle or other such firearm. Rifles are better than handguns if only one is available).

36. Boots * * * * * (I tie a good used pair of boots on my bug-out-bag).

37. Sheet of painter's plastic 10'x10' * * * * *

Very light weight but important piece of your gear. Use it for shelter, gathering water when it rains, wind break, solar still, sitting on to keep from getting wet, wrap around emergency covering. It packs easily and takes up very little room.

38. 3-4 feet of ¼" surgical tubing (solar still use) * * *

39. Small magnifying glass * *

40. Small foldable shovel or trowel (digging tool)

41. Small Bible * * * * *

Alan Corson

There are countless stories of people in life threatening survival situations who managed to survive because of their belief in God, family and friends. Religious faith can be a strong factor in any survival situation.

WATER

Water is the most essential element that you will need to survive. Many people will be able to survive for many days or weeks without food but your ability to function and survive without water is limited to only a couple of days or so. That length of time will be drastically reduced if you are in a very dry climate or if you are exerting yourself physically. In that case you may only have a few hours before you fall to the effects of dehydration.

The average adult requires about three quarts of water a day depending on their activity. The amount of water that you will need to sustain yourself in a survival situation, depending on the environment, is about one quart of water a day. That amount increases substantially depending on the degree of your physical activity. If you do not drink enough water you will get dehydrated.

What is Dehydration?

Dehydration occurs when the amount of water leaving the body is greater than the amount that is being taken in. Water is lost through body wastes, through the process of breathing, and from perspiration evaporated to keep the body at the proper temperature.

Dehydration can be deadly in either hot or cold weather. Dehydration from diarrhea and vomiting from drinking contaminated water result in thousands of deaths around the world each day.

What Are The Signs And Symptoms of Dehydration?

The body's initial response to dehydration is:

* Increased thirst—the body's signal to you that you need water

* Decreased urine output—the body is trying to conserve on water loss

* The urine will appear yellow in color

* Fatigue

* Muscle weakness

* Nausea

As the process of water loss increases more symptoms become apparent:

* A person begins to have a very dry mouth sensation

* The eyes stop making tears

* Sweating may slow or stop

* Muscle cramping will occur

* Increased nausea and vomiting

* Lightheadedness and dizziness

* Weakness

* Headache

* Irritability

* Flushed dry skin

* Excessive thirst

* Convulsions

* Low blood pressure

* Rapid and deep breathing

* Unconsciousness

* Death

As dehydration continues, the body tries to maintain proper cardiac function to pump fluids through the body. If the amount of water in the intravascular space is decreased, the body will compensate for this decrease by increasing the heart rate and by making blood vessels constrict to try to maintain blood pressure, and the flow of fluids to vital organs in the body.

The body restricts the flow of fluids from the skin to vital internal organs, which include the brain, heart, lungs, kidneys and intestines which causes the skin to feel cool and clammy.

The body's ability to cope begins to fail as the level of dehydration increases. When dehydration becomes acute the person experiences confusion and weakness as the brain and other vital body organs receive less blood.

If the person is not treated soon they will go into a coma with organ failure and death will eventually occur.

It is also important to avoid any alcoholic beverages when facing dehydration. Alcohol increases dehydration as the body must eliminate more fluids from the body than the amount of alcohol ingested. The body uses water to process the alcohol out of your system thereby increasing the state of dehydration.

In any survival scenario it is absolutely imperative that you learn to obtain water in the area where you are, and understand the ways to disinfect the water for consumption. Water is Life. You cannot go without it for very long.

Since water is so important to your survival you need to be thinking about collecting water as soon as you can. Even with all of your survival equipment, if you do not have the ability to collect, carry, and disinfect an adequate water supply you will die.

This cannot be emphasized enough. Water is absolutely essential for your survival. In any survival situation you need to immediately begin gathering and storing every drop of water that you can. Everything becomes secondary to your ability to obtain a supply of drinking water. Make this an absolute priority to your survival tasks.

Water To Drink

It must be said right here and now that in any given disaster or survival situation you must assume that any surface water is unsafe to drink without treatment. Disasters are notorious for destroying municipal water supplies and anyone drinking this water needs to take proper action to purify and disinfect the water before drinking. This also applies to any surface water that you may find out in nature.

You need to know that there is no such thing as "pure water." Even in the pristine mountains, all water in nature contains some impurities. When water flows from streams, and rivers it eventually accumulates in ponds, lakes and other bodies, and as it flows it filters through the various soils and stones in the ground. The water dissolves minute particles of these substances which accumulate in the water. At certain levels these contaminants make the water unsafe to drink.

More importantly, most surface water in nature contains nasty little microorganisms including bacteria, pathogens, and parasites, which if consumed will cause you serious illness. You can get Giardia, Cryptosporidiosis, dysentery, hepatitis and hookworms to name just a few of these nasty bugs from drinking untreated surface water.

When the water you want to drink may be riddled with microorganisms, parasites and bacteria, you cannot afford to be lax on water disinfection. You should always have more than one way to purify water in a survival situation.

Giardia is a nasty little parasite that causes intestinal discomfort, diarrhea and severe cramps that can last for weeks or even several months. If you get Giardia, in addition to being miserable for quite some time, it will limit your ability to travel and severely impair your ability to perform the necessary tasks needed to survive.

Cryptosporidiosis is a disease caused by a microscopic, single celled parasite. Symptoms include watery diarrhea and abdominal cramping. An infected person will commonly have vomiting and a low-grade fever. These symptoms normally last for about two weeks but may last for as long as a month.

Individuals who have compromised immune systems can suffer severe life-threatening complications with liver and gall bladder disease. Individuals receiving cancer treatment, those with HIV, and those taking drugs that suppress their immune system are most at risk. After being exposed a person may become ill in about 2-10 days. People generally contract this disease when they drink contaminated water or eat contaminated food with microscopic fecal matter containing the parasite. Individuals can also become infected after handling objects contaminated with infected human or animal fecal matter. Unwashed hands can then transfer the parasite to the mouth, infecting the person. People can also be infected by ingesting contaminated water while using waters such as streams, rivers, and lakes. This is not just a wilderness issue. There have been cases of people becoming sick after swimming in swimming pools contaminated with stools from infected persons.

Any of these nasty little bugs can leave you severely incapacitated. Vomiting and diarrhea from these microorganisms will severely dehydrate you and sap your strength to the point that you may not be able to perform the tasks needed to survive. So how can a person avoid contracting these diseases?

Assessing Water For Drinking

* Running water is normally purer than water that is not moving.

* Water emerging from the ground is normally purer than water that has been running over the land.

* Try to find clear water sources.

* Avoid water that has algae growing on it such as ponds and other stagnant water sources.

* Avoid discolored water if at all possible.

* Avoid water in marshes and swamps if at all possible.

* Try to locate where the water is coming into a lake or pond. It is less likely to have bacteria at that location.

Now a side note to consider: If the only alternative you have to drinking possibly contaminated water is to die, then you may choose to go ahead and drink the water and risk contracting an illness. If you can reach medical assistance, doctors can treat you for any of these waterborne illnesses, and you will likely make a full recovery. You may "wish that you were dead" if you get these waterborne illnesses but in the end modern medicine can effectively treat these illnesses for you.

Fortunately, we have methods we can use to effectively control these diseases before we get them. To further avoid these water borne illnesses you should:

1. Avoid water or food that may be contaminated. Do not drink water directly from rivers, streams, lakes, ponds, springs or any other unknown source. Assume that your drinking water is unsafe, and that it needs to be boiled or chemically treated before drinking.

2. Always wash hands with soap and water after using the toilet or getting your hands dirty in the soil.

These nasty little organisms generally get into water supplies when the source of water becomes contaminated by animal or human sewage. Surface waters such as rivers, streams, lakes, and ponds are more likely to contain these microorganisms than other ground water.

Always treat any surface water from the backcountry before drinking. All water sources away from city treatment facilities may be contaminated by unseen pollutants. Water sources in communities hit by a disaster should always be considered contaminated and should be purified before drinking.

Now, I know that you may come upon a remote, crystal clear cold mountain stream or pond that looks very inviting to a thirsty traveler. Visually the cool water looks crystal clear but there may be a host of unseen, very harmful parasites and bacteria in that water that will be hazardous for you to drink.

Always properly treat drinking water from any source in nature before drinking.

Boil The Water

Whether you are in an urban disaster or in the wilderness, the best method to kill bacteria, pathogens, and parasites in your drinking water is to boil it. There are several opinions as to how long you should have your water boil before it is safe to drink. The general rule is that you should bring your water to a rolling boil and maintain that boil for <u>at least one full minute</u> before you remove the water from the heat source, allow it to cool and then drink.

It won't hurt to boil the water for a longer period of time but if you are low on fuel in a survival situation and trying to conserve every bit of your fuel, you can use the one minute rule and that will in most cases sufficiently disinfect the water for drinking.

If you are in a stationary location and you have an adequate supply of fuel (such as wood) readily available to you then by all means go ahead and let your water boil for a few minutes (5-6 minutes or so would be enough) to be absolutely sure that your water is free from any bacteria, and parasites. Boiling your water for longer than this is of no additional value and is a waste of fuel and your time.

You probably want to cover the pot on the fire to allow it to quickly boil and retain as much of the water as possible and reduce evaporation. Once the water is boiled, let it cool in the same container. It can then be put in storage bottles when it is cool. Be sure to transfer the purified water into sanitary containers which have not been used to dip water from a lake or stream.

Always segregate the containers you use when boiling water. Always use a separate container for dipping into the water source from the container that you use to store your purified water. Never mix the functions of these containers.

It only takes a tiny amount of contaminated water to ingest the microorganisms that you are trying to avoid. Even putting your lips on the edge of a contaminated container to drink may be sufficient to introduce these microorganisms into your body.

After you boil your water for cooking you may find that it has a flat taste. This happens because the oxygen gets boiled out of the water. You can easily restore the taste to the water by pouring the water back and forth from one clean container to another. This replenishes the oxygen and taste.

After boiling the water to disinfect it for cooking, a person does not need to allow the boiled water to cool first before using it for cooking. Just be sure that you boil the water long enough to disinfect it before adding the food to cook. The important rule to remember is that you must bring the water to a rolling boil for at least one minute or longer to properly disinfect the water before using it for cooking. Some people make the mistake of adding their food to a pot of boiling water too soon, and contaminate their food because the water was not properly disinfected.

If you put food in contaminated water to cook, it gives germs a place to stay and they may not be killed in the amount of time needed to cook your food.

The biggest problem with boiling water for treatment in a survival situation is that you can't treat very much water at a time. You also need to be in a stationary location to build a fire and take the time necessary to boil and then cool the water.

You should be aware that even boiling the water will not remove heavy metal pollutants or chemical contamination in the water. If you boil your water but then taste the water and find a metallic or chemical taste you should refrain from using that water. Find another water source.

At this point it is very important to understand the need to carefully handle containers that you are using to purify water. Any container that has been exposed to surface water sources must be considered contaminated.

Remember, it only takes a drop of contaminated water containing parasites, bacteria or pathogens to make you very sick. Wash out all containers with bleach or other suitable sterilizing solutions to sanitize them before use. If possible, boil water in these other metal containers to sterilize them. Failure to follow this practice will eventually result in you getting the very illness that you are trying so hard to avoid.

Water Filtration

The first step in preparing your water to drink is filtration. This is simply running the water through a clean cloth to remove large particles suspended in the water. This is the first step before proceeding with the disinfecting process. Filtration does not disinfect the water or make it safe to drink.

Filtration is especially important if you are going to be using chemical disinfection because disinfectants are less effective in water that is cloudy, murky or that has suspended particulates. The disinfection chemical bonds to these particulates and can reduce the effectiveness of the disinfection.

You can filter the water by using a clean cloth such as a white sock, clean T-shirt, pant leg or other suitable cloth which allows the water to pass quickly through multiple layers of cloth.

Plastic Bottle Filter

One way to quickly and easily filter water before treatment is to cut the bottom out of a plastic container such as a beverage bottle or other such container. Roll the cloth up and then stuff the cloth into the container and into the neck of the beverage bottle. Pour the water through the filter, out the neck and into another clean container. The water should be clear when passed through the cloth filter. The water is not purified at this stage and is NOT ready to drink! You have simply removed the larger particles from the water in preparation for further treatment.

If you want to filter water while you perform other chores, just improvise and hang your beverage filter on a tree limb or sturdy bush with a catch container directly underneath. Pour the water into the filter and allow the water to slowly filter and fill the container as you perform other chores.

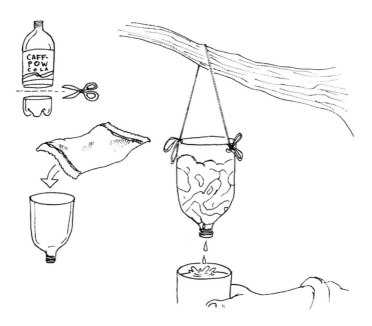

The best way to filter water in a survival situation is to use the layering method. Use whatever materials that are available to you such as cloth, clean sand, charcoal from your campfire, pebbles, and larger stones. Put the smaller materials at the bottom and increasingly larger materials toward the top of your filtering system.

Tripod Water Filter

You can use the tripod water filter in either an urban or wilderness environment. This device can easily be made using three sticks about 3-5 feet long depending on your circumstance.

Tie them together at the top with the **cordage** in your bug-out-bag to make a three legged teepee. Then tie three or more layers of filtering inside the tripod. Place these filtering materials beginning at the top with the larger materials and then smaller materials as you work your way down. Place a container on the ground inside the tripod to catch the filtered water.

Pour water into the top filter cloth and as the water moves down it will pass through increasingly fine materials to filter the water and remove large organic particles, debris and sediment. Remember, the water is now filtered but not disinfected. At this stage it is not ready to drink.

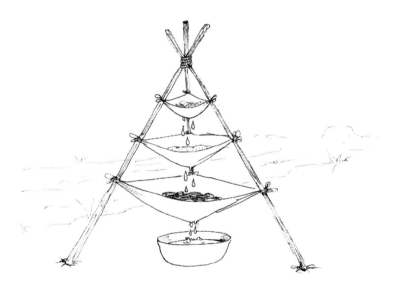

One effective way to treat any questionable drinking water is the use of a special commercial water disinfecting device that processes the water to make it drinkable. These commercial devices are a light weight disinfecting system which normally uses a pump and filter material which is capable of trapping Giardia, and other harmful bacteria and parasites before you drink the water.

When using these devices you simply put one end of the hose into the water source and pump the unit until potable water flows out the other end of the hose. The special filters trap any harmful microorganism in the water. The water is then ready to drink.

You can find a wide variety of commercial personal water disinfecting systems in stores. Filtering the water before you use the personal water disinfecting device is important to eliminate the larger contaminants such as bugs, scum, decomposed leaves, sediment and other debris.

Water filters for this purpose are normally rated in "microns." Since different pathogens come in different sizes, you want to make sure that the water filter that you purchase for your bug-out-bag filters out the smallest bugs or the tiniest microns.

The downside to these filtration systems is that they can be bulky, expensive and when these filters become clogged you must clean or get new filters to continue purifying your water. It won't take long to clog these filters when you process water from a muddy river or small mud puddle. Most of these filter systems are mechanical and things with moving parts are subject to breaking.

The "LifeStraw" water filter is an excellent water filter system that has no moving parts. It is inexpensive and will effectively remove Giardia and Cryptosporidium and other microorganisms. It filters up to 1,000 liters (264 gallons) of water. It removes 99.9999% of waterborne bacteria and 99.9% of waterborne protozoan parasites. It filters down to 0.2 microns. It is an excellent water filtering system that is lightweight and easy to carry. I carry one in my bug-out-bag.

Again, if at all possible, be sure to always strain the water or filter it through a piece of cloth to get rid of the heavy organic and inorganic particles suspended in the water. This will substantially enhance the water filtration process and your filter will last longer.

Iodine Another good way to make your drinking water safe is with the use of iodine tablets (Potable Aqua) or solution of iodine (Polar Pure). Iodine is an inexpensive and easy way to purify water. Iodine is lightweight and hardly takes up any space in your bug-out-bag. Be sure to read the label on the Iodine since you will need to wait 30 minutes after treatment to allow the iodine to work. Iodine can be less effective in cold or murky water. Be sure the iodine solution you use guarantees on the label that it is effective against Giardia.

If you are using 2% Tincture of Iodine, use five (5) drops for every one quart of water for most water sources. Jostle the water some to mix the chemical and then let the water sit for a full 30 minutes before drinking the water.

If the water you are trying to treat is not clear, and you are suspicious of this water, add up to ten (10) drops (maximum) of iodine to treat a quart of water. You will also need to allow the treated water to sit for an additional 20-30 minutes for the iodine to do its job. If the water is extremely cold you need to let the treated water sit for at least two hours before use. The water will taste strongly of iodine when the process is completed.

The advantage of purifying water with iodine is that you can purify water while on the move. Just add iodine to a container, put on the lid and continue your journey allowing the iodine to work in the water for at least 30 minutes before drinking.

Remember, when you want to drink the iodine treated water be sure that you squeeze or slosh some of the treated water from the bottle and allow the water to spill over the mouth of the container and run onto the container's lid/threads to effectively remove any microorganisms that may be trapped in the lid or on the lip of the container. It only takes a tiny amount of contaminated water to make you very ill.

Use 20 to 40 drops of iodine per gallon of water depending on how clear the water is and let it sit for a full 30-45 minutes. Do not repeat the dose. If it doesn't smell like iodine with the first try, throw it out. Find another water source.

When you are treating your water with Iodine make an effort to use warm water. The iodine is more effective in warm water than it is in cold water.

For very cold water increase the waiting time after mixing the iodine to 1-2 hours.

Liquid Tincture of Iodine 2% solution has a shelf life up to several years longer than the iodine tablets that are available in stores. Iodine tablets are quite inexpensive and they are susceptible to moisture and heat which will degrade their potency. Either product is widely available at most drug stores or pharmacies. Be sure you check your bug-out-bag every six months to a year and replenish the iodine or other chemical treatment tablets as necessary.

Another excellent use of iodine is its use as a disinfectant for the treatment of minor wounds. Just apply the iodine to the wound to disinfect.

You should know that pregnant women should not use iodine drops to purify water as it may have an adverse effect on the fetus.

There are some downsides to using iodine to disinfect your water. Taking in too much iodine over several weeks can suppress your thyroid gland and make you really sick. It also makes the water taste bad. Iodine can have adverse health consequences in people with thyroid disease, and individuals who have shellfish allergies.

When treating your drinking water with Iodine you may experience a mild unpleasant taste to the water. This is to be expected. If you decide to add some additive to the water and that additive contains vitamin C (ascorbic acid) this will act to neutralize the iodine before the iodine completes its work to kill the pathogens.

You need to wait the full 30 minutes (or longer) after disinfecting the water before you add the flavoring to the treated water.

You should consult your doctor to see if Iodine is appropriate for you to carry to purify your drinking water in an emergency situation.

Disinfecting small amounts of water

Chlorine Bleach Another method of helping to purify your drinking water is to use ordinary <u>unscented</u> household bleach. You need to use plain old liquid chlorine bleach, (sodium hypochlorite—5.25%—6% strength).

You can carry this in a small 2 ounce plastic droplet container that you clearly and boldly marked as "Bleach." The bleach should be 5 to 6 percent sodium hypochlorite with no preservatives or other additional ingredients.

It is important to not use scented bleaches, powdered bleaches or bleaches that have added chemical cleaners. Also do not use any bleach that has fragrances or perfumes. The good news is that bleach is a common chemical found all over the world. It is easy to find and inexpensive to purchase.

Again, before bleaching your water always strain or filter the water through a piece of cloth to get rid of the larger organic and inorganic particles. This will substantially enhance the bleach chemical treatment of the water.

Treating water with bleach is effective at killing most germs, and it doesn't taste different to most of us because this is basically what most city water supplies purify with. You want the chlorine bleach that smells like chlorine. This bleach is now available in different concentrations. There are several brands that will work. Ultra Clorox is a 6% sodium hypochlorite solution instead of 5.25% but it is still chlorine bleach. Keep a 2 oz. plastic droplet bottle of 5.25% or 6% chlorine bleach with no additives in your kit for water disinfection. Refresh the bottle's contents every six months to a year if you don't use it since bleach loses potency fairly quickly.

To treat water with chlorine bleach, put the filtered water in a clean container and add 3-4 drops of chlorine bleach to one quart of water. If you are using liter containers use the same dosage. Jostle the container some to mix the contents and then let the water sit for 30 minutes. When ready to use, slightly open the cap and allow some purified water to run over the lip of the container and into the cap/threads. This helps sanitize the container's lip and cap where a small amount of contaminated water may have been trapped.

The treated water should smell like chlorine. If the treated water does not smell like chlorine add an additional 1-2 drops of bleach (per quart / liter) and let the water sit for another 30 minutes. For very cold water add the wait time to 2-3 hours to allow the chlorine to work.

Always follow the rule when using iodine and chlorine to treat water. If the water is cloudy or if in doubt, add a bit more chemical to the water and let the water sit for a longer period of time before drinking. It's better to add a bit more chemical and wait a little longer than to rush the project and get sick.

For larger treatment use 12-16 drops of bleach for every gallon of water. Shake the mix lightly and let the water stand for 30 minutes. If the water does not have a little smell of chlorine, repeat the dosage with an additional 8-10 drops per gallon and let it sit for another 30 minutes. If it smells slightly of chlorine it is now good to drink.

If it doesn't smell of chlorine after two treatments, the water is too dirty to use. Throw it away and treat a new batch of water from a different water source.

Be sure to check the strength of the bleach you are using. If the strength of the chlorine you have is only 1% then use 45 drops per gallon or 10 drops per quart. If the chlorine strength is 7-10%, then use 4-5 drops per gallon or one drop per quart.

Chlorine-releasing compounds cannot be depended upon in semi-tropical and tropical regions. In these instances boil the water or treat with iodine for best results.

Here is the formula for treating water with Chlorine Bleach having 5.25%-6% strength:

BLEACH FOR DIFFERENT WATER CONTAINERS	
1 quart bottle	3-4 drops of bleach
2 liter bottle	6-8 drops of bleach
1 gallon jug	12-16 drops of bleach
2 gallon cooler	¼ teaspoon of bleach
5 gallon bottle	½ teaspoon of bleach

You should know that there is conflicting information from the medical community regarding the ability of sodium hypochlorite (bleach) to effectively kill Giardia and Cryptosporidium. There are those who claim that it does and there are those who claim that it does not. Many people have used bleach successfully to treat their water but if you have any concerns that either of these parasites are in your water you should always boil the water before drinking.

Solar Water Treatment

You can disinfect water by using the sun. After you filter the water through a cloth to remove larger particles, pour the water into clear plastic containers such as quart size containers. Make sure all labels are removed to allow the maximum amount of sunlight to contact the water. Put the cap on and place the bottles in direct sunlight for at least 6 hours. This process obviously would be more effective in sunny environments.

This process can eliminate harmful microorganisms through ultraviolet radiation and heat from the sunshine. Research indicates solar treatment can disinfect water from such sources as rivers, streams, ponds, and lakes. This process will not remove harmful chemicals, commercial pesticides or other toxic metals from the water. You should also use smaller containers since sunlight has a more effective penetration in shallow water.

Where To Find Water?

In a survival situation around your home, improvise and search those places where water may be found. Here are a few possible sources for water around the home.

* Home hot water heater—probably holds 50 gallons of fresh water

* If you are on a private well, your well house may have a 50-80 gallon container of fresh water.

* Home toilets—holding tank

* Garden hose—lying on the ground that has not been drained

* Underground sprinkler system—even when drained water remains in the pipe

* Water line to your home—may be able to access and drain water there

* Flower pots or other containers in the yard or garden

* Rain gutters

* Water fountains

* Fish ponds

* Fish aquariums

* Any depression in the ground that has trapped rain water

* Small puddles or ditches holding water

Carefully search for any small nook or crevasse that may have caught rain water. This water may be found around stones, masonry, trees and in shaded areas where small pools of water may have been trapped.

If you are in your home environment you will be very familiar with other surface water sources such as rivers, streams, lakes and ponds near your residence. If close enough these may be sustainable water sources that you can use for extended periods of time.

Try to avoid water sources that have heavy chemical treatment such as golf course ponds and holding ponds around chemical plants or businesses. While you may be able to disinfect this water by ordinary means, you probably will not be able to easily remove toxic chemicals from this water.

In any survival preparation you should always store containers of water in your home for an emergency situation. You should plan on about one gallon of water per person per day, although you can reduce that a bit in a survival situation depending on your environment. You should have at least enough water at home for you and your family to last 7-10 days. You should always have a means of collecting additional water to use.

The easiest way to store water at home is to designate certain containers just for that purpose. You can buy 5 gallon water storage containers from most camping or outdoor stores. These are excellent for water storage. These containers can be heavy when full so you won't want to be moving them around much. Store these containers in one convenient place at home. You can also use ordinary milk containers, plastic beverage containers, or water bottles. The smaller bottles are much more portable especially in a survival situation. Glass containers are good but glass has a tendency to break so I would stay with good plastic containers for water storage.

Even though you are using fresh tap water, you still need to purify this water for long term storage. This is easily done with ordinary chlorine bleach. Be sure to use the unscented type bleach. This stored water will be good for six months or so and then it is best to replenish the water. Use the listed bleach formula to preserve your water depending on the size of the container. Store this water in a dark place to prevent algae from growing.

If you suspect that you will lose electricity in a pending storm, turn up the temperature dial in your refrigerator and freezer to the coldest setting. If you lose power try not to open these appliances until absolutely necessary. A closed refrigerator or freezer will keep the food much longer than one that is repeatedly opened.

For long term power outages wrap your freezer and refrigerator with large blankets to insulate them from the warmer outside temperature. The food in these appliances will last longer.

If the power is suddenly lost at your home, turn off all major appliances. This will reduce any "power surge" that may happen when the power is restored. Sometimes this power surge will damage or even destroy your appliances. Computers, sewing machines and similar appliances with advanced electronics can be especially susceptible to power surge damage. After the power is back on you can begin to turn on your appliances when it is clear that you have steady uninterrupted power.

Every year thousands of people die in their home from hypothermia. Many die in severe storms after their home has a power outage. Simple preparation could prevent many of these deaths.

Generator

A portable gasoline generator is an excellent tool to have available to you in any disaster where you will be staying in your home. A generator will allow you and your family to continue to have some electricity in your home even if the power grid is down for days or weeks.

A generator can keep you warm, preserve your food, and provide some light for your home. A small generator (2500-4000 watt) can provide these services and is relatively inexpensive to purchase. They operate on standard gasoline fuel.

If you use a generator make sure that you place the generator in a safe location with plenty of ventilation. Generator engines create toxic exhaust fumes that can kill you. Make sure these exhaust fumes cannot seep into your home.

The best plan is to be able to connect your portable generator directly into a special electrical circuit that provides power to some of your home's electrical devices. This can be done by connecting a special heavy electrical cable from the generator's plug outlet into the special home electrical circuit. This special circuit also prevents generator electricity from "back feeding" down the line where it could potentially injure someone.

Since the generator is small and portable it cannot provide all of the electrical needs of your home. That's okay because all you need is to have some heat, light and cooling to keep the contents of your refrigerator and freezer preserved. You will find that you can be very comfortable with just a little bit of electrical power.

You may be running your generator off and on for several days after a disaster. You will need to plan for a continued source of fuel. Before a storm hits you can fill your ordinary fuel containers and use them to replenish the fuel in the generator when it gets low on gas.

If a major disaster hits you will find that fuel is as precious as gold. There certainly will not be enough to go around and everyone will want it.

Another good plan for emergency gasoline is to keep the gas tanks on all of your vehicles full. Keep the fuel tanks in your lawnmower, boat, recreational vehicles, and extra fuel containers you have full before a pending severe weather event. When the storm passes you can easily use this fuel in your vehicles so you are not storing unnecessary fuel in your garage at home.

Siphon Gas

In an emergency, a resourceful person can cut a 6' length of garden hose and use that to siphon gasoline from your vehicles. Use caution when siphoning gas using this method to insure that you do not drink or inhale gasoline as this will cause serious health problems.

Fuel siphoned from vehicles can be stored in gas containers which then can be used to fill the generator or used in your gasoline camping stove. Most vehicles have around 20 gallons or so of fuel and that will last a considerable length of time. You may want to keep a 6 foot length of ¾" clear polyurethane plastic tubing in your home survival kit for just this emergency purpose. The advantage of the clear polyurethane tubing is that you can see the gasoline as it gets close to your end. That allows you to quickly drop the end of the tube into a container to allow the fuel to flow. This helps prevent you from getting gasoline in your mouth.

In many disasters if you find yourself in an urban survival situation for an extended period of time, you should be able to scrounge around and locate additional plastic fuel containers. It may be possible to locate abandoned vehicles to siphon gasoline from their tanks to provide the fuel you need to survive. Try to keep your fuel containers full. Do not wait until you are completely out of fuel to begin searching for your next fuel source. This should normally be done discretely. For obvious reasons you do not want to attract attention to the fact that you are getting fuel from abandoned (or not so abandoned) vehicles, and other sources.

Survival Ladder

Whether you are preparing for a survival situation from an urban disaster or just live in a 2-3 story home, it is a good idea to have a way to escape if your home catches on fire. This is especially critical if you live on the upper levels.

In many disasters it is common for gas lines to be broken, flammable fuels spilled and downed power lines sparking all around, all of which create a rich environment for dangerous house fires.

You can purchase (or make your own) second or third story survival ladder and store it under a bed for rapid use. These should only be used if fire blocks the normal exits to leave the home.

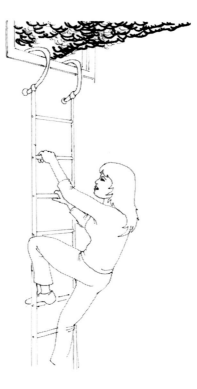

In an extreme emergency if you are upstairs with children, do not have a ladder to get them safely out and have no other way to safety, you can use a length of rope. Tie a secure loop in the rope and place it under the child's arms snugly. Put on a pair of heavy leather gloves and then lower the child out the window and safely to the ground. If the child is heavy you can reduce the pull by placing the rope on the window ledge and allowing some of the tension to be taken by the rope on the window sill as you lower the child.

Have someone on the ground remove the rope and attend to the child while you retrieve the rope for any other children who need to be saved. As the last person out, you can lash the rope securely around a heavy dresser, metal bed frame or other solid object and then lower yourself out the window to safety. These safety items should always be immediately available in each room upstairs. You may not be able to leave a room to get these items if a fire occurs.

Disaster Plan—Home & Away

It is always best to have a disaster plan for staying at home, and another disaster plan for evacuating your home to travel to a safe location. Everyone in the family must know what to do if the family is not together when a disaster occurs. They need to know where to meet if a disaster happens, and a specific location where the family will travel to in the event you need to leave your home.

You will not be able to rely on contacting family members by cell phone since emergency cellular telephone calls will quickly overload the system preventing you from making or receiving a call.

A good survival plan will significantly reduce the fear and anxiety if a disaster should happen. It allows everyone to know ahead of time what they must do and where they are to go. Review these plans and the various travel routes with the family frequently.

Warnings To Leave The Area

If you do get advanced warnings of a severe weather event and authorities are directing people to leave their homes, it is important that you follow these warnings in a timely manner.

All too often we see instances where people have ignored repeated warnings to leave their homes. They stay behind thinking they would be safe only to be hit with the disaster and then need to be rescued.

Many of these individuals are needlessly injured and killed simply because they failed to comply with official warnings to leave. In many disasters the resources of emergency personnel are strained to the limit and there will be occasions that rescue personnel simply cannot get to a person in time.

It is not only important to keep your vehicle's fuel tanks full for a home fuel supply, but a sudden change in a severe storm warning may require you to quickly leave your home to travel a distance to reach safety.

You may be traveling substantial distances or get caught in heavy traffic leaving the area which will cause significant congestion and delays. You need sufficient fuel in your vehicle in the event you are caught in heavy traffic. Gas stations on your route may be out of power or closed. You do not want to run out of gas on this trip to reach safety!

If the power is out, listen to weather reports on your **hand crank radio** for NOAA weather reports for your area. If you need to leave, have all emergency supplies prepared and ready for immediate packing so you can leave quickly.

Be sure you have a safe route that you can travel to reach your destination since roads can get blocked, bridges get washed out, and highways get damaged making them unusable. Always have several backup routes planned.

Assisting Others

You should always try to help a neighbor who may have a special need or require special assistance in a disaster. These include the elderly, people with infants or those with other special needs. Offer assistance to insure that they are able to safely stay in their home when appropriate or by helping them to collect the things necessary for them to safely evacuate.

It is likely that your family, friends, and neighbors will know that you have made preparations for disasters long before a disaster happens. They may seek you out to ask your advice on what they need to do in a survival situation. Always take the time to offer your assistance to help. Your advice may save a life.

Try to contact friends and family to let them know of your travel plans. Better yet, give a copy of your disaster plans to family and friends who live outside your area. With this plan they will already know what you are going to do, and where you are going if you need to suddenly evacuate your home after a disaster.

If you decide to leave your home be sure to leave a note in a conspicuous place to let other family members, friends and rescue personnel know that you have left. This note should be as detailed as possible providing information on the date and time you left, where you are going, names of individuals that are with you, when you expect to arrive at your destination, what means of transportation you are using, and if possible the route you expect to take. Provide emergency contact telephone numbers on this note.

Outdoor Water Source

If you find yourself in an outdoor wilderness survival situation away from home, the first thing to do after you are in a safe location is to make a good effort to look for any water sources around you. You may be able to easily see rivers, streams, creeks, lakes or ponds from your location. Listen carefully for the sounds of running water. Look for green vegetation, which frequently grows close to water sources.

Even if you find yourself in a survival situation without any obvious water source around you that does not always mean that you cannot obtain water to drink.

Snow—Melting for water

If you are in an area where you have access to snow or ice you can obtain emergency water to drink. To effectively melt snow, select the snow from the cleanest area possible. Put a small amount of snow into your pot and then put the pot onto the fire. Ideally you want a bit of water in the bottom of your pot before you add the snow to keep the bottom of the pot from scorching. It is better to add smaller amounts of fluffy snow into the pot rather than packing the pot with large amounts of snow.

When melting snow you will find out very quickly that it takes a lot of snow to get even a small amount of water. You will see that hanging a snow packed pot over the fire will usually just result in burning the pot and giving a bad taste to any water that you get.

Clean snow is made up of the purest of distilled water that can come from the atmosphere. It is wonderful to drink. If you feel the snow/water is unsafe to drink for some reason, just continue to boil the water for a minute or so and then let it cool.

Be sure that you do not use contaminated water to brush your teeth, or wash your pots and pans. Remember, it only takes one drop of contaminated water to make you very sick.

People often ask if they can eat snow to satisfy their thirst or if this will lead to reducing the core temperature of the body.

The answer is that you can eat snow when you are thirsty. The only caution is that you do not want to eat snow if you are in an extreme cold environment and your body is struggling to keep warm. You will know this if your body is shivering from the cold. Also don't eat snow if your body is overheated in hot climates. However, if you are walking through an area with snow and you are warmly dressed by all means eat some snow to help satisfy your thirst.

Water From Ice

Melting ice to get water is much more efficient than melting snow. Getting water from ice falls into the same category as other surface water . . . it needs to be disinfected before drinking.

Cold weather does nothing to destroy bacteria, parasites, or pathogens in the water. The ice only suspends these nasty little bugs for long periods of time.

If you come to a frozen lake, stream or river you may have to chisel a hole in the ice to access the water below. If at all possible you want to get to the water since it is easier to get drinking water from liquid than is it from processing drinking water from ice.

Harvesting Rain

Harvesting rain can be an easy and effective way to gather drinking water. Just lay out the large piece of plastic or a tarp from your bug-out-bag to catch water.

Use a stick, soil or other similar objects to curl up all sides making a basin to prevent the water from escaping. The garbage bag in your bug-out-bag makes an excellent water catching device. You can cut the bag so the plastic is fully extended and then lay it out to collect water. This plastic can be used over and over again to collect water and for many other survival uses.

You can also harvest water from rooftops, and gutters. Be aware that water from this source may contain considerable contaminants and toxic materials such as bird droppings, and roofing material toxins. Be sure to filter and properly disinfect this water before drinking.

I am always amused whenever I see a house with a huge blue tarp draped over a large section of the roof. I always wonder if the roof is actually leaking or if that family is just very progressive in harvesting a large amount of their water supply by diverting roof water into ground cisterns.

For those proactive individuals who are interested in being prepared, it would be good to have a large tarp for your roof to be able to divert rain water into large containers. Depending on your environment and your annual rainfall, you may be surprised at just how much water can be harvested in this manner.

Morning dew

Dew is small water droplets that form in the early morning and late evening hours. Dew forms when the temperature of a surface is low enough to permit moisture from the air to condense on it. You can capture morning dew that has formed on vegetation or exposed surfaces.

Condensation is the same process that occurs when you take a cold glass bottle of your favorite beverage out of the refrigerator and set it on the counter in your warm home. Soon moisture droplets (water) will form on the glass bottle.

Dew can be collected from most cold non-porous exposed surfaces with a clean cloth. Just wipe up the moisture and then squeeze the cloth and allow the water to flow into a clean container. If necessary, just squeeze the cloth allowing the water to drip into your mouth.

Another method of collecting morning or evening due is to tie pieces of clean cloth around your ankles and legs. Walk through any tall weeds and other vegetation that is covered with dew and the cloth will quickly soak up the moisture. Squeeze the moisture into a clean container for drinking.

Finding Water Close to the Sea

In a survival situation you may be able to obtain water in the sand dunes above the ocean beach. Look for an area well above the high-tide water mark of the ocean. Look for areas where the sand appears moist and dig to locate water in that area. This may be found in depressions behind sand dunes on the beach.

You can try waiting until high tide has partially passed and then dig a hole below the high tide water line. If there is any fresh water available you will find it on top of the heavier salt water in the hole. You only want to dig the hole until the first signs of seepage occur. You will need to filter this water before disinfecting it for drinking.

It is very important that you do not drink sea water. Water from the sea will further dehydrate you and if you consume enough it is actually poisonous. Drinking sea water will cause significant problems for the kidneys, which can stop functioning and result in your death.

Water At Sea

Obtaining fresh water to drink at sea can be very difficult. Getting fresh water to drink in rough seas is even a more difficult proposition.

The easiest way to obtain drinking water at sea is to collect it from the atmosphere when it rains. Be prepared for any such occurrence so that you can quickly and easily collect as much rain water as possible. During any rain, drink as much water as you can and then quickly store as much as you can for later use.

Use anything that will catch and hold water such as the 10' x 10' piece of plastic in your bug-out-bag. Spread this out as much as you can and turn up the sides so you can catch water when it rains. If you see clouds forming be prepared for any possible shower or squall.

Boat sails will soak up or hold water in the event of a shower. Use boat sails and tarpaulins and other such material for shade and have them ready with turned up edges in case you encounter a sudden shower. Use any cloth that you have, even your clothing to catch water. When the cloth gets saturated just squeeze the water into a container or into your mouth.

You can collect water from early morning or evening dew or if a fog happens to rolls in. Dew and fog will form on surfaces that you can wipe with a cloth.

In a survival situation you can get some moisture from fish at sea. Catching and eating birds that attempt to use your boat/raft as a perch will also help satisfy your thirst and hunger.

If available, you can process sea water with a desalting kit. These kits are typically used only for immediate need when you have extended periods of overcast weather when solar stills are not able to operate. You can also try to make a solar still, which will give you fresh drinking water from sea water.

In any survival situation you may have gone without water for a long time and you will be very thirsty. When you are finally able to get water be sure that you do not make the mistake of suddenly drinking a lot of water to quench your thirst. If you do, you will likely get nauseated and will vomit. When you have access to plenty of water take your time and drink small sips of water and extend that to an hour or so. Relax knowing you have plenty of water to drink. Enjoy the wonderful feeling of drinking fresh water and rehydrating your body.

Arctic Environment

We all know that the arctic has massive amounts of ice and snow. There is plenty of water available. The danger is that in this extremely cold environment, eating snow and ice can kill you.

In extreme cold weather your body is battling to maintain its warmth. Eating ice and snow in these conditions will lower the core temperature in your body, which will cause you to dehydrate. This can lead to your death. In these extreme cold conditions it is highly recommended that you always melt snow or ice on your fire before drinking it as water. It is best if this water is warm or mildly hot when you drink it to allow your body to absorb some of this heat.

Some may mistakenly believe that a person needs less water because you are in a cold arctic environment. This is not true. You will actually need more water to survive in extreme cold conditions because your kidneys must work overtime to eliminate body waste, which are ordinarily handled by sweat glands.

If you do not have a pot or other suitable container to melt ice or snow on your fire, you can improvise and use a T-shirt or other cloth material. Just wrap a packed ball of snow or ice in the cloth and hang it on a stick close to your fire. The heat from the fire will melt the ice or snow and you can catch the water in a plastic container. If you do not have a container you can allow the cloth to get saturated with water and then squeeze the water directly into your mouth.

A small pit can also be used in a survival situation to get water when you do not have a pot, cup or other container to catch water. Dig a small hole and then pack the sides tightly with snow with special emphasis on packing the bottom of the hole. Then put a pile of unpacked snow into the pit. Take a hot stone from the fire and use a stick or other object to move the stone into the pit. The heat from the stone will melt the fluffy snow. Quickly removed the stone and drink the water. Repeat this process until your thirst is satisfied.

Other Water Sources

Water in forests and in areas along the sea are generally found closer to the surface and will be easier for you to access. Normally this requires very little digging to produce some water.

Fresh water seepage is common if you dig in the proper location.

In other situations digging for water is physically demanding and you do not want to spend a lot of time and energy digging for water in a location that offers little sign of producing water for you.

When searching for water do not overlook those areas where water has run seasonally through canyons, deep creeks or ravines. The beds may be dry at that time and water may not be visibly present but it is possible that water may be running beneath the surface. Search for low areas that show signs of moisture and dig there for water.

Search on the outside of a bend in a ravine possibly shaded and where green vegetation is growing. Dig in that low area and you may find a water source.

If you locate any dry pond, lakebed or other seasonal water source, look for the lowest area and then try digging for water there. Often times the water will be just below the surface in this area where it can be accessed.

While green vegetation is not a certain sign that you will find water at that location, it does serve as a valuable guide for finding water. You want to dig out any patch of lush green vegetation where there has been a seasonal spring or creek of running water. You are likely to find water in that area.

If you encounter an area with lots of stones be sure to search for hidden springs and areas of water seepage among these stones. This area may produce water sources in cool shaded areas with nearby vegetation.

Sometimes you may find tiny pools of water hidden down between large stones. Although this water may be only a foot or so away, its location between large boulders may appear impossible to reach. You can use your **3-4 foot surgical tubing** as an improvised straw to reach this water. Alternately, you may be able to push a piece of cloth into the crevasse to soak up the water. Squeeze the water into your mouth or into a container if it needs to be disinfected.

You are also able to find water on mountain tops where permanent snow banks are located. You must evaluate whether it makes sense to climb to the top of that mountain to find a water source or save your energy and look for water in more accessible places.

The Solar Still

The **piece of plastic sheeting** you have in your bug-out-bag that you used to harvest rain water (and can be used for shelter) can also be used to obtain water from a solar still. This simple lightweight plastic can save you from dying of thirst.

In a desert environment you can use a 10' x 10' piece of painter's plastic sheeting to accumulate up to 1-3 pints of water in one day. If you only have a 6' x6' piece of plastic that will work too.

The solar still works by collecting potable water from the condensation that is produced from green vegetation. You can also use non-potable water or just moisture from the ground to get potable water from the solar still.

First dig a hole in the ground that is about 40" wide and 24" deep. For a 6' x 6' piece of plastic dig a hole about 24" x 24".

Place a clean container such as your bug-out-bag's **pot, cup or pan,** at the bottom, and center of the hole.

Fill the hole with green vegetation. You can even put in a second container in the hole filled with undrinkable water such as saltwater or even urine.

Place one end of your **3' length of surgical tubing** from your bug-out-bag into the clean container, and lay the other end of the tubing out of the hole under the plastic where you can access it later.

Cover the hole with the sheet of plastic. Anchor the plastic all the way around the edges with dirt. You want to seal the plastic all around the hole but you do not want the plastic to be tightly fitted over the hole.

Place a stone in the center of the plastic so that the plastic will sag in the center directly over the clean container.

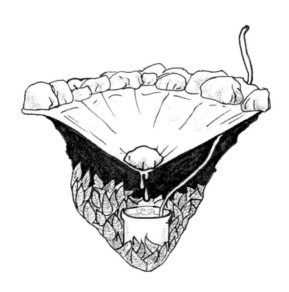

The solar still operates when the sun's heat shines through the plastic and evaporates water from the vegetation (or from the saltwater or urine in the second container). In this process it will distill the undrinkable water making pure water vapor. The vapor condenses on the cooler underside of the plastic, and drops will flow down the underside of the plastic's "V" and drip into the clean container.

After the distilled water has collected in the clean container at the bottom of the hole you can use the 3' long surgical tubing like a straw to drink the water from the container without disturbing the still.

If you don't have surgical tubing just lift one part of the plastic sheeting to reach in and get the clean container. The water in the clean container is now drinkable without any further treatment. Drink that water and then replace the container to continue the distilling process.

It is important to set up the still if at all possible so that you do not need to remove the plastic very often since it will take about half an hour or more for the air in the still to become resaturated to begin the distillation process all over again. If in a desert environment and you have access to cactus, pulverize the green vegetation before tossing it into the hole. This will help the distillation process extract the water from the plant.

Transpiration for Water

A variation of the solar still is a process called Transpiration. It is essentially a process of obtaining water from plants through evaporation. It is easy to do and requires very little time or energy. You will need one or more **plastic bags** from your bug-out-bag or other sources.

Take a plastic bag and place a small clean stone on the bottom in a corner. Then place the bag over the leaves on a bush or tree and then tie off the end of the bag. You want to use lush green leaves for this process.

The sun heats up the interior of the bag causing water to evaporate from the green leaves. The water will condense inside the plastic bag. The water droplets will flow down to the lowest part of the bag (where the stone is located).

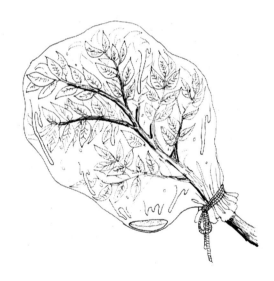

Water droplets may cling to the underside of the plastic bag so when you want to access the water shake the bag a bit to get as much of the water down to the bottom as possible.

The nice thing about transpiration is that it takes very little time or energy to set the bags to collect water. The downside of this technique is you will need to be in a stationary location long enough to allow the process to work. Also, this method will likely render only a very small amount of water in each bag. The more bags you set out, the more water you are likely to capture. Parenthetically, depending on your environment, your body may actually use up more water in the time that it takes to collect water using only this method.

Note! Be careful that you do not use this process with any poison plants (poison oak-poison ivy) or coniferous (Pines) or vegetation that have glossy or shiny leaves such as apple, oak, or maple as these may cause cyanide poisoning.

Urine . . . Can You Drink It?

This is a survival question that almost always comes up in any survival discussion. The fact is that you can drink urine as a last ditch effort to survive. Humans have been doing this for thousands of years in survival situations. There are important rules to follow.

Human urine is not poisonous, and is in fact sterile. You will not die or become ill if you drink it.

Here is what is important to remember:

* In a survival situation you need to drink the urine as soon as possible after you pass it.

* Do not attempt to store urine for later use as it is likely to become contaminated.

* Do not drink urine more than <u>one time</u> since the urine becomes so concentrated with body wastes that the kidneys are not able to process it and you can develop renal failure, which can kill you.

Keys to Finding Water to Drink

It is important that you use all of your senses when searching for water. Carefully look to see where any wildlife goes to get water. Animals must have water and will generally go to a water source at least once a day. Many game trails eventually lead to a source of water. Look for game trails that fork together as these will likely head in the right direction where water is located. These game trails generally tend to go downhill. The sight and sounds of birds can be an indicator of a water source. Birds that feed on grain will often congregate near water holes, or other sources of water.

If you happen to get caught outside in a sudden rain shower, quickly take advantage and get your bug-out-bag's plastic sheeting, tarp, mess kit containers, plastic bags, and even use your clothes to soak up rain water to later squeeze out into a container or into your mouth if that is all you have to use. Use anything at your disposal to catch rain water to drink. After you have satisfied your thirst then begin to fill all of your containers with water for later use. Water is vital. Never pass up a chance to restock your supply.

When you do find an adequate source of water be sure to properly disinfect the water and then drink until your thirst is completely satisfied. In any survival situation it is important to nourish your body with plenty of water when you have it. It is even good to continue to drink some water even after you are no longer thirsty. This adds vital water to your system and your body will eliminate any excess that it does not need. Just don't overdo it and drink water until you become ill.

Plants are an excellent way to locate possible water sources and to let you know if the water is good or not to drink. If you locate a pool of stagnant water, check for plant life nearby. If there is no plant life there is a good possibility that the water is bad. Avoid that water source. If you see plants that are thriving in that area, the chances are that the water is good to drink.

Avoiding Dangers Near Water Sources

It is important to understand that remote water sources are used by all types of wildlife.

When locating these water sources be mindful that other animals including potentially dangerous animals may use this same source of water.

You may encounter these animals coming to the water source or leaving the water source at any time of the day or night. Some predators use water sources to hunt for prey that frequent these areas. Use caution when approaching or leaving water sources to avoid any dangerous animals.

If you are in an environment that has alligators, crocodiles, hippos or other similar dangerous game, use extreme caution as you use rivers and marsh areas where these animals live. In these environments you are just another food source for these predators.

Also, be careful around remote water sources since you may encounter dangerous snakes that frequent these areas both for water to drink and to hunt small game that frequent there.

Choosing The Right Knives

A good knife in your bug-out-bag is an essential tool for your survival. Knife-like tools have been used for the past two and a half million years. Knives have been made from stone, bones, obsidian and flint. Knife blades have evolved from bronze, copper, iron, steel and ceramics.

The blade on most knives extends into the handle either partially, which is known as a "Stick Tang," or they extend the full length of the handle. Tangs that extend the full length of the handle are often visible on the top and bottom. Knives with full length tangs are generally considered to be stronger than "stick tang" knifes.

The weakest point on a knife is generally either the blade tip or where the blade tang meets the handle.

If your knife breaks during a survival situation you are at a serious disadvantage. It is pointless to purchase a cheap survival tool that will not hold up when it is needed.

Fortunately, there are many different companies that manufacture knives which will serve you well in any survival situation. Many of these quality knives can be purchased without bruising your pocketbook.

Knife blades are manufactured from a variety of materials. Each of these materials has their own advantages and disadvantages.

Knife handles are also made from a wide variety of materials and each has their advantages and disadvantages. They come in a wide variety of shapes and styles.

You want to purchase a knife that fits your hand comfortably, and has a blade design suitable for your needs. Various types of knife handles are available and here are a few:

- o Wood: Good grip but does not resist water well over time. May crack or warp with prolonged exposure to water and heavy use.

- o Plastic: Easy to care for, durable, but may be slippery when wet.

- o Rubber: Are generally preferred over plastic for their durability, good gripping qualities and cushioning.

- o Micarta: Very popular due to its toughness and durability. Good in water and offers good grip when wet. Many varieties of this material are available.

- o Glass Reinforced Nylon (GRN): High strength, impact resistant.

- o Skeleton Handles: These are knives that use the tang as the handle. These handles are usually wrapped with parachute cord or other similar wrappings to enhance the grip. When gutting animals the parachute cord can become saturated with blood and is hard to keep clean and sanitary.

- o Aluminum: Many grades. Good general purpose use.

- o Carbon Fiber: Very strong and lightweight material.

- o Kraton: Much like rubber. Very good hand grip qualities, weather resistant.

Blade Steel

GOOD:

These knives are your basic "entry-level" stainless steel knives that are typically manufactured in Asia. The blades on these knives have an adequate edge holding ability and are rust resistant. These knives offer a good value. The steel in these knives are softer when compared to higher grade steel, and they will require more sharpening.

The blade examples are:

- o 420

- o 440A

- o 7Cr13MoV

BETTER:

The better grade of stainless steel blades have higher chromium content but are more expensive. These blades offer a better edge holding capacity and require less maintenance than blades listed above. The blades are fairly easy to sharpen with ordinary sharpening tools. These blades offer a very good value and performance and are very good for everyday use.

- o   AUS6
- o   AUS8
- o   440C
- o   8Cr13MoV

BEST:

The best stainless steel knife blades are made in the United States and Japan. They are excellent blades but come at a higher cost. These knives have superior edge sharpness and require less sharpening. They have very good rust resistance. The quality of these blades make them ideal for demanding jobs.

- o   CPM 154
- o   S30v
- o   VG-10

Knife Blade Patterns

Drop Point is a pattern used on many knives and is commonly found on hunting knives. The tip is lowered (dropped) with a convex arc from the spine. This allows the tip to be ground thicker.

Clip Point is a great all-around format and one of the most popular. The blade shape uses a concave or straight cut-out towards the tip. This is an excellent all around use knife for survival purposes.

Sheepsfoot The spine curves down to meet with the straight edge. They can be used safely as a rescue knife or in situations that don't require a point. Not normally considered the first choice for an all-around survival knife.

Spear Point is a symmetrical grind with the tip being in the center of the blade. Double edged, the spear point shape makes the dagger. This blade would not do well in skinning applications. Not considered good for all-around survival situations.

Tanto This knife blade is identifiable by the shape that is angular, using two straight edges that are joined. The tip on this format is very strong due to the spine keeping its full width until it nears the tip. The tip then tapers to create the point. This is another good knife design but will not be the best for skinning applications. Not considered a good choice for all-around survival use.

Straight Edge blades are the standard for general knives and cutlery. They provide an edge that will cut cleanly and be sharpened easily. These blades are a good choice for hunting. This is a very good design for an all-around survival knife.

Fully Serrated blades are good for cutting fibrous material but are not blades that perform well in skinning and all-around survival applications.

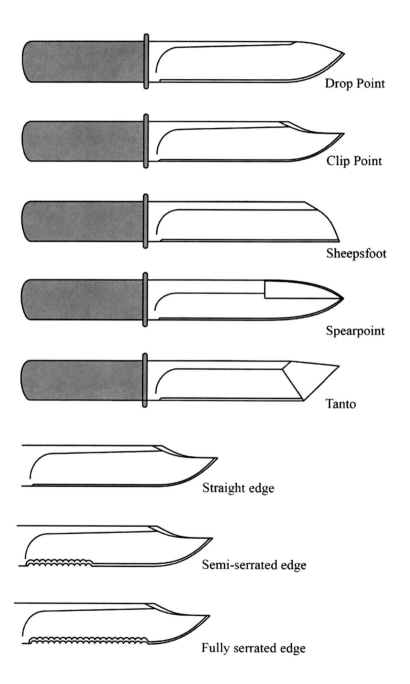

FIRE

In a survival situation, fire is generally the most basic need after water. Fire gives you the ability to boil and disinfect water for drinking. It will give you warmth to enjoy a safe and comfortable night out. You cook your meals with fire and dry your clothes with it, which in cold climates can quickly mean the difference between life and death. You use fire for signaling for help. You should never venture out at any time without the ability to quickly light a fire in an emergency situation.

If you experiment with some of the fire making techniques described in this book you will very quickly realize the importance of carrying a good lighter or other modern means of starting a fire. Many of the fire starting techniques described in this book may require hours of labor to successfully accomplish. Unless you are able to carry fire with you, you will have to repeat that laborious and time intensive process all over again when you need your next fire.

It won't take long pounding two stones together trying to make a spark to make you wish you were carrying a good lighter. Always carry a modern means to start a fire. If you are ever suddenly faced with a survival situation you will be glad that you have it.

Gather your various fire starting materials and practice with them in different conditions to see what works best for you.

You will find that you like certain fire making materials better than others. What is important is that you don't wait until you are suddenly faced with a survival emergency to begin learning how to do things that could save your life.

Building Your Fire

While there are countless ways to build a fire, the principles of making a wood fire are the same. Fire is initiated by a spark that sets tinder, kindling and then larger fuel burning.

Starting any fire, especially under survival conditions, must be performed with deliberate thought, and careful attention to fire making details. You will spend a lot of time and waste precious survival resources if you haphazardly go about attempting to start a fire. This is particularly important when it is very cold out and you need to quickly build a fire.

Begin by collecting and preparing all of the necessary items to make the fire. You will be much more successful starting a fire if you attend to detail, and not simply rush to set a match to some wood.

Having your bug-out-bag **fire starting kit** will greatly aid your efforts to build a fire. Your bug-out-bag contains all of the necessary items to start a fire such as your **butane or Zippo type lighter, fire steel striker, magnesium bar, wooden or paper matches.**

Butane Lighters:* * * * * These are wonderful fire starters since they instantly give off a full flame rather than a spark that needs nurturing. These lighters operate on vaporized butane.

One problem with butane lighters is that butane evaporates at about—0.5 Celsius / 31.1 degrees Fahrenheit. The lighter will likely not function well, if at all, below these cold temperatures since the butane will not vaporize properly. Generally you can warm the lighter up by putting it into your pocket for awhile allowing the butane to again light.

Magnesium Bar Fire Starters: * * * * * The magnesium fire starters are an excellent way to start a fire in a survival situation. They are very safe and won't burn in a solid state. To use them scrape along the side of the bar with a knife to make a small pile of shaved magnesium on top of your tinder. Then turn the bar over and use a knife or piece of hacksaw blade (which normally comes with the magnesium bar) to quickly scrape the ferrocerium rod causing a burst of sparks to cascade into the pile of magnesium shavings and tinder. The magnesium shavings will flare up and begin burning very hot. Immediately add secondary tinder and then kindling to get your fire going. One magnesium bar will light hundreds of fires.

Zippo Style Lighters: * * * * * These are lightweight refillable metal lighters. These lighters operate in harsh weather and are not subject to the temperature limitations of butane. The lighter uses a lighter fluid, wick and a small stick of flint. By thumbing the lighter wheel you get a very nice flame even in very cold weather. This lighter is good for thousands of lights as long as you keep it filled with lighter fluid and replace the small flint when it is used up after hundreds of lights. Many people store 2-3 extra flints in the base of the lighter along with an extra wick.

Steel Fire: * * * * * These are special metal rods that when scraped with a sharp object, such as a knife, will produce a shower of very hot sparks. You hold the fire steel rod on top of your tinder and hold the knife against the rod. Pull up quickly on the rod and a shower of sparks will light the tinder on fire. By pulling up on the rod rather than pushing down on the scraper you will not knock over your pile of tinder. After lighting just add more tinder and kindling to start your fire.

These tools can be used even when completely wet. They will strike a hot spark anywhere in any weather. One fire steel can easily make hundreds of fires.

Paper matches:* * Although these matches are commonly carried by many, they are generally not a reliable fire starting source for survival purposes. Paper matches and their striking surface can easily become wet from the weather or just damp from perspiration rendering them useless.

If paper matches are all you have in a survival situation, take immediate action to protect them from dampness. Wrap them in aluminum foil, a piece of plastic or put them into some type of weather resistant container to protect them. This should also be done with any wooden matches that you have in your kit. Paper matches also need a striking board to light them. Keep the match striking board dry as well.

You will also need some type of tinder to initiate the fire. Here are some types of tinder that you can make yourself or purchase. Be sure to keep a good stock of tinder in a waterproof container in your bug-out-bag.

Tinder

Tinder is simply lightweight highly flammable material that will catch a spark easily or take a flame to start a fire. You can improvise in a survival situation and use items such as pocket lint from your clothes, or strands of cloth from slightly torn cloth. Twine, rope, tampons, and items from a medical kit such as gauze and cotton bandages work well as tinder. You can use bits of hair, dry grass, punk from dead wood, bits of dry tree bark, dry moss, dry animal dung (buffalo dung was used extensively by the plains Indians for fire to warm their teepees) and anything else that you can find that will burn long enough for you to add larger kindling to your tinder.

You may be able to enhance any tinder in a survival situation adding very small amounts of flammables such as solvents from firearm cleaning kits, gun powder, gasoline, diesel, and even charcoal from your previous campfire to help the tinder become more flammable. Extreme caution needs to be exercised whenever you are using any highly flammable substance around fire.

A good way to start a fire in the wild is to locate a bird's nest. These nests usually contain dry sticks, down and feathers and are good sources of tinder. In caves look for dried bat droppings as this provides a good source of tinder. Locate a cedar or birch tree and pull small strips of bark to shred and break up for tinder. Termites commonly found in so many environments produce fine pulverized wood that when dry makes very good tinder.

You will likely use whatever wood that is available to you in a survival situation. The various softwoods will split easily and quickly turn into a crackling fire. Softwoods such as white cedar, red cedar, spruces, Douglas fir, and pine will quickly start a fire but produce less heat than hardwoods. On most softwood trees the small dead sap filled branches found near the bottom of the tree are excellent and will burn vigorously to start your fire.

Softwood will typically burn hot and fast but will not last through the night. To bank a nice fire that will keep you warm through the night you need to add some hardwood to your fire. Hardwoods like oak, hickory, maple, beech, birch, and ash are excellent for long burning overnight fires.

If you find yourself in a survival situation where everything around you is covered with a heavy coating of ice do not worry, you can still get a fire going. Remember that most softwood trees have small dead sap filled branches found near the bottom of the tree. Gather these and break them up into small sticks, the sap in these small branches will burn easily and you will soon have a nice fire going. Split smaller limbs with your hatchet or knife to get to the dryer wood inside. Dry this wood out by the fire. Be sure to save some sap filled twigs for your next fire.

Plants Used To Make Tinder

If you live in an area where cattails grow you can scrape the brown heads of the plant to get the very dry fluff that will burn fairly well. Even when this plant is wet you will still be able to get dry fluff from the inside of a cattail head. Parts of cattail are also good to eat.

If you have Milkweed or Fireweed available in your area, you can open a pod to find lots of fine hair like fibers which can be used as tinder. Incidentally, these are plants that you can also eat.

If you are ever in a survival situation be sure to look for suitable tinder as soon as you can. In the forest look for anything dry that will serve as tinder.

If you find tinder that is wet, put it into your pocket where it is warm and allow it to dry out. You can also dry out wet tinder for later use by placing it close to the fire.

Tinder You Can Make

Cotton balls * * * * * coated with Vaseline or other similar petroleum product are excellent for this purpose, and they will even burn in light rain or snow.

Dryer lint * * * * * that is plain or lightly covered with candle wax is another source of excellent tinder that is free for the making, lightweight, easy to pack and easy to use.

Char cloth * * * * is cotton material that is decomposed by heat to make tinder. The process is called "Pyrolysis." This process works as you separate an organic substance into a solid and gas by high temperatures in an environment that is free of oxygen (inside the tin). You need the fire on the outside of the tin and a lot of heat inside the tin. The small hole in the lid allows gases to escape. Be sure that you do not overcook the cloth in the fire. Overcooking allows oxygen to get in the tin through the hole in the lid, and it will then burn the cloth.

Making char cloth is very easy. It basically involves taking small pieces of cotton material (such as a t-shirt) and cutting it up into several 3" pieces. The exact size is not important.

Put the pieces loosely into a metal container such as an Altoids tin. Even a tuna, shoe polish can or many other similar containers will work. In a pinch you can even use heavy aluminum foil as the container.

The lid (or aluminum foil) needs to have a small hole in it to allow gasses inside to escape. You can secure a lid on a tuna can or other tin by using a small piece of thin flexible wire (snare wire will work) to wrap around the container's lid to hold it on tightly. If you use a side cutting can opener the lid will sit nicely on the container.

Put the tin into the coals of your fire and you will soon see smoke streaming from the hole in the lid. When the smoke stops (after about 5-6 minutes depending on your fire, the amount of cloth inside and the container) the process is finished. Safely remove the tin from the fire/coals, and you should see black charred pieces of cloth inside . . . char cloth.

A piece of char cloth will easily catch a spark and glow embers. If you blow on the char cloth embers they will grow and you can then add the char cloth to other tinder to make your fire. Char cloth is very useful because it takes the tiniest spark to create an ember that smolders long enough for you to add more tinder to start your fire.

The thicker the cotton material the better the char cloth will be. Keep your char cloth well protected in a small waterproof plastic container since it will dissolve if it gets wet. Do not use anything that is synthetic to make char cloth as this will simply melt in the container.

Fat Wood: * * * * * Fat wood is pine wood that has a heavy concentration of sap or pitch. It can readily be found around evergreen woods. Fat wood or "pitch wood" is usually found in dead conifer trees where their sap has condensed into particular areas of the wood.

Fat wood is easy to recognize as it has a honey-like appearance with a strong smell of pitch when brought close to the nose. When handling fat wood you will immediately notice the soft sticky sap on your fingers.

You can use your **survival knife** to pry into the tree to cut a chunk of sap wood out. You can use your knife to split this large chunk into smaller pieces for igniting your fire. This sap filled wood really burns good! You can use fat wood to quickly build a fire when you have to use damp or wet tinder.

Whenever you happen to find fat wood in your travels be sure to put some extra pieces into a plastic bag in your bug-out-bag for later use. It is an excellent fire starter. Fat wood can also be purchased commercially if you are not in an area where it is easy to find.

Other Tinder

* Commercial stick fire starter bars * * * * * (very good but expensive)

* Candles (small candle stubs work well) * * * * *

* Cedar Sticks (shavings to start fire) * * * *

* Cedar shavings with candle wax * * * *

Important Things To Remember:

Choose the location carefully where you want to start a fire. Ideally you want an area that offers an adequate supply of fuel for your fire. Having a water source close by is an added benefit.

- o   Check the wind to be able to shelter the area where you want to start the fire.

- o   Assess weather conditions to determine a good place to build your fire.

- o   Gather all of the necessary tinder, secondary twigs, kindling and larger wood before starting the fire. Always gather more wood than you believe that you will need. It's always better to have some wood left over for the morning brew than have to get up in the middle of the night to search in the dark for wood to re-stoke your fire.

- o   Look for an area that has natural objects that can be used as a wall near your fire such as large stones, fallen trees, soil banks or even snow banks. These are useful to reflect the heat back from your fire.

- o   Do not start your fire directly on the ground. Use a piece of dry bark, some small sticks, stones or other dry material as a base to make an elevated area to start the fire. An elevated base protects your fire from moisture in the soil. It also allows oxygen to feed under the flames to give your fire a boost. A fire built on an elevated base will focus the heat upward and not so much into the ground.

The sides of this base will also help protect the fire from any breeze when first started.

Sometimes it may be necessary to start your fire in a slight depression or hole in the ground to protect it from the wind. Always try to put down a base to start your fire no matter where it is started.

o   No matter what type of fire starters you have, be sure that you prepare all of your tinder, secondary twigs and larger fuel before you strike the match or spark. When using matches make a concerted effort to make that first match count. You never know for sure how many other fires you may need and in a survival situation every match counts.

o   If you are in need of rescue, try to start your fire in a location that can easily be seen by others who may be searching for you either on the ground or from the air. A fire deep in the woods may have the smoke diffused by the tree canopy and will be difficult to see from the ground or air. A fire in an open area will allow the light from the fire and the smoke to be seen from a distance.

Cutting Wood For A Fire

You have a **hatchet** in your bug-out-bag which will make chopping wood for the fire much easier. The small pieces that you get when chopping firewood are excellent to use as tinder and kindling. If you don't have a hatchet available, you can make fire wood by using your large knife to split sticks. If necessary you can use another stick as a club to tap down on your knife blade to split pieces of wood and small logs.

If you have nothing else you can simply snap pieces of wood with your hands, wedge a stick between two stones or trees and pull or push to break it. It is not recommended that you place a stick up against an object and jump on it as you may accidently injure your leg or ankle in the process. Preventing injuries is critical in any survival situation.

If you are in a situation where all of the available wood is wet, find the driest sticks that you can and then remove the bark. Split the wood with your hatchet or knife. Generally the center of the stick will be dry. Cut the outside bark off the stick to introduce as much dry wood to the fire as possible. Try to find wood that has been sheltered from the rain. Look for wood from the underside of a dead leaning tree. In areas where trees have blown down find wood that has been protected by other fallen trees. When you get your fire started place other firewood nearby to dry it out for later use.

Stones To Make Fire

If for some reason you find yourself in a situation where you do not have any modern means of starting a fire, you must improvise. Look around your area to see if you can find stones such as Obsidian, Quartzite, Agate or Iron Pyrite.

One easily recognizable stone that you can use to make sparks is iron pyrite, which is also known as "fools gold." This stone appears to have small flecks of gold embedded in the stone. These and other hard stones will work to create a spark by striking the two stones together over your tinder. This may be difficult and will take some time but with patience you should be able to make sparks that will set your dry tinder on fire.

Metal To Make Fire

If you scrounge around in an urban environment you can find some type of metal to use to make sparks for your tinder.

Hold the metal closely over your prepared tinder and strike down flatly with a knife blade to send a few sparks into the tinder. If you do not have a knife, you can use any steel or iron to strike the other metal to create a spark. You will need to practice this process depending on the metal you have to get the correct technique to make sparks for your tinder. Sometimes this can be physically demanding and takes a long time. Remember the motto: **Never Give Up!**

Battery & Steel Wool

You can easily start a fire with a battery and roll of fine steel wool. A 9 volt battery works well in this application but any similar battery or the electrical system on any car, boat, aircraft, recreational vehicle or other motorized vehicle will work too. The composition of fine steel wool is such that the current from the battery quickly superheats the steel wool. Just cut off a piece of steel wool from the roll. Make a piece about 6"-7" long and ½" wide. Put the steel wool on top of your tinder and then rub the steel wool on the battery's two terminals. When you see the steel wool begins to glow and then burn, remove the battery and coax the steel wool into a flame by gently blowing on it. The steel wool will catch your tinder on fire. The finest steel wool is "oooo" grade, which is the best to use.

In a survival situation if you have a cellular telephone you can use the cell phone battery in the same way with steel wool to start your tinder on fire.

If you do not have any steel wool to use you can still use the battery to start a fire. Take two short scrap pieces of wire (you can use the wire from any small appliance such as an old lamp cord, vehicle engine wires, aircraft wiring, home wires or almost any other similar wire). Bare the ends and connect one wire to the positive battery terminal and the other wire to the negative battery terminal. Then touch the bare ends of the wires over your dry tinder. The wires will spark into the tinder starting it burning. If necessary, you can simply use paperclips, safety pins or other similar metal. Just hold them to the battery with one hand, and use your other hand to touch the ends together to get a spark.

In cold weather be sure to keep the battery inside your clothing where it will stay warm. Cold weather quickly drains the power in a battery. Also, do not expose the battery to extreme heat such as the desert sun. Extreme heat may cause the battery to explode. Protect the battery from any rain or moisture. Water will destroy the circuitry in a battery.

Glass Lenses

You can make a fire with a magnifying glass.

Some of us may remember as a youth that if we were lucky we could find a small toy plastic magnifying glass prize in certain packages of Cracker Jack popcorn. When confined to my bedroom on a sunny day (for whatever I did wrong . . .), I would enjoy using that tiny magnifying glass with the direct sunlight through the window to make newspaper burn. I was lucky that we did not have smoke detectors back then as I would have surely been discovered. At the time, confined to my room, it seemed to me that I was in a "survival situation." For those of you who have used a magnifying glass to melt ants on a hot summer day as a child, well, you will know how to do this . . .

To create a fire with a magnifying glass, simply pinpoint the sunlight beam on the area of your tinder. A magnifying glass, binocular lens, eyeglass lens or wristwatch crystal will all work for this purpose. If you add a bit of water to the lens you actually intensify the focus of the beam to start your tinder on fire faster. This only works when you have sunlight. If it is overcast or dark out you will need to improvise another way to light your tinder on fire.

Ammunition

If you are a hunter or have access to ammunition you can use the gunpowder to ignite your tinder. Carefully remove the bullet from the cartridge and pour a small amount of gunpowder on top of your tinder. Strike a spark over the gunpowder and it will quickly flash creating sparks to ignite the tinder on fire.

You can also use a very small amount of gunpowder with stones to create sparks to light your tinder. Just sprinkle a small amount of gunpowder on a fist size stone. Take another similar size stone and aggressively grind them together directly above your tinder. The gunpowder in the stone will ignite causing sparks to fall into the tinder.

Fire From Ice

When I first learned of this I thought that it was one of those "survivor tales" that looked good in the movies but was not actually possible. The fact of the matter is that you can actually start a fire from a sculptured piece of clear ice. You just need to form the ice into a lens shape, and then use it in the same manner as a magnifying glass. This takes time and practice but it comes in quite handy in a survival situation in icy weather.

First of all the ice needs to be clear. If the ice is from cloudy water it will not allow the sunlight through to work.

You can improvise and make your own ice lens. Just fill up a cup or other small container with clear surface water or melted snow. When the ice freezes you are ready to begin making the lens. Take a block of ice that is about 2" thick. Use your knife to shape the ice into a lens. The lens should be thicker in the middle and thinner toward the edges. When the lens is properly shaped, polish the lens with your bare hand. The heat from your hand will further melt and sculpture the lens into a nice smooth surface that will allow the sun to penetrate.

You are now ready to use the lens to start your tinder on fire. Put the lens close to your tinder and allow the sun's rays to penetrate the lens and focus the sunlight on top of the tinder.

Use gloves or other suitable material to keep the lens from melting in your hand and water dripping onto your tinder. When your tinder begins smoking and develops embers, blow on the embers gently until they develop into a flame.

This method takes time and practice. When you accomplish starting a fire with ice you will have a great feeling of success!

Fire Thong

You can make a fire using a 2-3 foot length of dry rattan about a quarter inch thick. Take a long dry stick about the size of your fist. Split one end with your hatchet or knife. Slip a piece of wood in the split to wedge it open a few inches.

Place a bundle of dry tinder in the base of the split allowing enough room behind it for the rattan thong. Hold the long stick between your legs and then begin to rapidly move the thong back and forth. It may take some time but the thong will heat up and eventually it will transmit heat to the tinder. When small embers appear in the tinder immediately gently blow on the tinder to allow it to grow into a full flame. Have your other fire starting materials close by so that you can quickly transfer the tinder bundle to small kindling.

While there are many different ways to start a fire when you do not have any matches or a lighter, most of these fire starting techniques are quite difficult to master. They are even more difficult in a survival situation. These techniques may look easy while thumbing through a survival book on a nice sunny afternoon. However, they are much more difficult when you are faced with a true survival situation working at night or when it is raining or snowing and when you are trying desperately to build a fire to keep warm.

Most of the time you will have difficulty finding the appropriate materials, your hands will be cold and wet and you will not be sufficiently familiar with these items to get a fire started.

Many people attempting these techniques will simply not be able to get a fire started. For this reason I have deliberately not included these advanced and difficult fire starting techniques in the book. It is better to take the time when you are not in a survival crisis to learn some of the more advanced fire starting techniques. Enroll in a good survival class, and then practice making these tools using various woods. Practice making fire with these tools, and develop the skills necessary should you ever need to use these methods to start a fire in an emergency. Sometimes it will take several days or longer to master these skills. When you are suddenly faced with an emergency survival situation is not the time to begin learning these fire starting techniques.

The Bow Drill

The bow drill is a method of fire-making that is the easiest method for beginners to master. This is not to say it is easy to start a fire using this technique because it is somewhat complicated with the necessary equipment. However, the equipment is fairly easy to make with the required materials. This method also requires some physical effort and patience.

The bow drill consists of a sharpened wooden spindle that stands in a hole on a fireboard. This is held in place at the top with some type of hand-hold material such as a piece of wood, bone or rock. The wooden spindle is rotated back and forth rapidly with the use of a bow string. The bow is simply a curved piece of wood with a piece of cordage (string) attached at each end.

Materials Needed

1. A flat piece of wood about one inch thick and a foot long. The wood should be a dry soft wood. There are many types of wood that will work depending on your location. You can use most Willows, Balsam Fir, Cedar, Poplars, Aspens and Spruces to name just a few. Use your knife or hatchet to split a piece of dry wood to make this board. You want the flat board long enough so you can place one foot on it to hold it in place while working the bow and spindle.

2. The spindle stick is made out of the same material as the flat board. The spindle is about 1" thick and anywhere from 6" to 12" tall. You will spin this spindle rapidly with the bow to create friction in a hole in the flat board.

3. The spindle handle is a palm size piece of wood or other material that you hold in your hand. This can be a piece of wood, bone or smooth indented rock that simply protects your hand and holds the spindle in place as it is spinning. If you have anything that can be used as a lubricant put some on the handle to reduce the friction between your hand and the top of the spindle as you work.

4. The bow is simply a curved stick about arm's length that has a piece of cordage tied to both ends. The stick needs

to be strong but still flexible. You do not want to use a stick that is old and brittle or it will break. The cordage does not have to be tight as you want some flexibility to be able to wind the spindle into the cord.

5. The cordage can be anything from animal leather, paracord, twine, heavy string or other suitable material.

Make the Spindle

Find a straight dry branch about a foot long that does not have any knots. Use your knife to whittle it into about a 1" round diameter. Whittle one end of the spindle into a somewhat blunt point. Carve the top of the spindle into more of a sharp point to reduce the friction near your hand.

The Palm Handle

Use your knife or hatchet to form a piece of wood roughly the size that will fit nicely into your palm. In the center use your knife to carve an indentation where the top of the spindle will set. A smooth rock with indentation or large bone will also work.

The String

Use whatever material is available to you with the string length about one and a half times the length of the bow. It is very important that the string is tightly wrapped around the spindle for this process to work.

Making The Bow

The bow should be from a green branch about 1" thick that is free of knots. It can be either straight or have a slight natural cure. It should be about two feet long. The limb should be strong and a bit flexible but not flimsy. Cut around the ends of the bow about an inch from the ends. Tie the string to both ends of the bow. The string should be a bit loose so you can attach the spindle.

Prepare the wooden platform by placing the spindle onto the wood base near the end of the board and about an inch from the edge. Use your knife to trace around the spindle. Carve a round indentation into the wood base. This indentation should be about an inch from the edge.

To use, kneel down with your foot on the wood base. Load the spindle by wrapping the string around the spindle so it is tight inside the bow. The spindle should be in the center of the bow. The spindle should now be tight in the bow string but not so tight that it causes it to break.

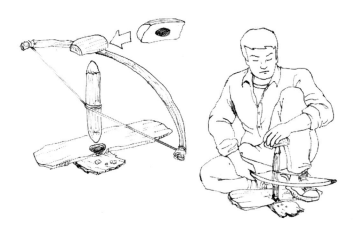

The top of the spindle should be held by the carved hand piece.

Beginning

Begin by moving the bow back and forth slowly at first. Keep pressure on the top of the spindle with your hand. This forms the spindle into the carved hole and will "burn in" the wood base.

It may take some time for this to happen . . . continue spinning the spindle as it begins to match up with the hole in the wooden base. Do the drilling for several minutes.

As you continue working to spin the spindle it is about this point in the process that you may feel a slight soreness in your hands, arms and back. You may begin telling yourself "this would be a lot easier if I just had a lighter on me." See? You are already learning good survival techniques! But for now . . . . continue with your drilling. Eventually you will begin to see tiny wisps of smoke at the end of the spindle.

After the wood base has been burned in, the next step is to cut a notch in the wood base immediately in front of the burned hole. This is done to allow an area for the grounded powder that you are creating to accumulate. Make a 45 degree cut to the top of the board to the center of the burned hole. Cut out the "V" in front of the hole.

Making the Coal

Place a dry material under the base "V" to catch a hot coal. You can use a small piece of bark, dry leaf, scrap of paper or any other suitable dry material.

As you use the bow drill you should see some light powder developing in the notch. Continue the process as the powder builds up. When you see ample powder in the notch, rapidly spin the spindle. You want the heat to make a coal from the powder. As you rapidly spin the spindle you should see an increasing amount of smoke. When you see a good amount of smoke from the powder for several seconds you will likely have a good coal. You need to gently blow on the coal until it is glowing. When the coal is glowing you can transfer it into your prepared tinder pile. Blow gently on the coal in the tinder pile to ignite the tinder.

Feather Sticks . . . Fire starters

You can quickly and easily make "feather sticks" or "fuzzsticks" to move your fire from tinder to kindling. These are easy to make and will certainly be worth your time when trying to start a fire under adverse conditions.

Feather sticks are made by simply taking a small dry stick and using your knife to shave down and around the stick several times to make wood curling on the stick. The wood curls remain attached to the stick in a "wave." You should make several of these before you begin your fire. The small finger size sap filled limbs from evergreen trees make good feather sticks.

Put three or four feather sticks on top of your tinder at the bottom of your prepared fire materials. The feather sticks should be angled upward so that they can easily catch a draft when the fire begins to burn. The open wave of the curling on the stick will quickly catch a flame and burn long enough for the other kindling to catch fire. Make a teepee with small dry kindling on top of the feather sticks for your fire. This allows oxygen to flow into the bottom of the fire to quickly ignite the fuel. Be sure to leave an opening at the base of the teepee so you can easily add another feather stick or two or small split kindling to the fire. Always have a few extra feather sticks on hand so you can immediately add them to a fire that is reluctant to burn.

In some dry conditions you may be able to just use several feather sticks to start your small kindling on fire without the use of tinder.

One thing to remember about making fires, large fires burn large amounts of wood. It takes energy to scout around to locate and carry wood back to your fire. If you take the time to properly locate your fire, there is very little reason to have a huge roaring fire (unless you are using the fire to signal for help). Make a smaller fire and enjoy the comforts of sitting close to the fire relaxing, and not spending your time and energy running out to locate more wood.

The Fire Can

This little stove will warm your food, heat your tea and is a great hand warmer on a cold winter night.

You may want to have a small, convenient but long lasting stove in your kit. This stove is simple to make and you can use a variety of containers such as shoe polish cans, tuna cans or other similar cans to make this stove. You will need some thin cardboard (corrugated is fine too) which is cut as wide as the can is tall. Roll the strand of cardboard up tightly until it fits into the can. After the can is full, take a lighted candle and drip candle wax all over the cardboard until the tin is almost full. Let the wax cool and harden.

When you want to light your fire can just set a flame to the cardboard and wait until it catches on fire. Be patient as it may take some time for the wax/cardboard to light.

If you used a side cutting can opener just put the lid back on to snuff out the flame. You can use this fire can several times before it runs out of fuel. Then just repack and reuse.

Types of Fires to Make

In all survival situations you need to save your energy. You can expend a lot of energy gathering, chopping/splitting wood. One way to efficiently keep your fire going is to simply feed large branches or long limbs/logs into the fire. Lay larger limbs or logs with one end into the fire. As the logs burn just push them further into the fire. Be sure that you closely monitor the fire since this method allows the flames to extend beyond a defined fire pit.

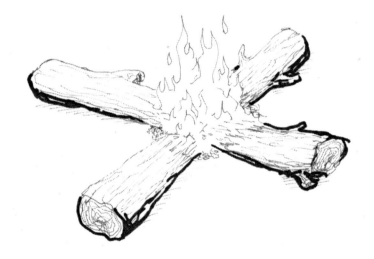

Dakota Pit Fire

A Dakota Pit Fire is another simple and efficient way to make a fire. This system can be used when you are short on wood fuel and you need a good fire that will keep you warm and you can cook on. Here is how to build a Dakota Pit Fire:

- Begin by digging a hole about 8" wide and 12" deep.

- Dig a second hole about a foot away from the first hole depending on the soil type. Dig this second hole in the same direction of the wind. The second hole should be about 6" wide. As you dig down about 6"-8" then curve the second hole toward the first hole.

- Connect both holes with a tunnel.

- Lay some dry twigs/sticks, dry leaves or a flat stone to make a base at the bottom of the first hole. Add some small broken twigs and shavings in the hole that will easily begin burning.

- Start your fire above ground and then push the burning materials into the first hole. To get the fire burning, blow air into the second hole feeding oxygen into the fire pit.

- Feed small twigs from the second hole into the fire pit to get a good fire going. This keeps a lot of wood from protruding above the ground. (Or you can just simply add wood into the fire pit from the top).

When the fire is going you can lay a couple of green sticks across the fire pit and then place your pot over the fire.

This type of fire is very good when you have limited wood available to use. The fire pit maximizes the use of the wood fuel since it is concentrated in the hole. It is also good when you need a fire in an area with high winds. This fire can also be used in a survival situation when you do not want to be seen.

Trench Fire

Another method of building a fire similar to the Dakota Pit is to simply dig a rectangle trench. The trench should be about 8-10 inches wide, a foot deep and two feet long. When the fire is burning in the trench just put some green sticks across the fire and set your pot over the flame. The trench is long enough to put several containers over the fire to boil water and cook your food. The open trench makes it easy to insert additional wood while the fire is burning. The trench fire operates with the same principles and benefits as the Dakota Pit fire to conserve on fuel and reduce visibility.

Reflectors For Your Fire

While there are many ways to build a fire, you normally will want your fire to give you warmth and allow you to cook or disinfect water. You may build a different type of fire that is designed to keep you warm all night. You will in most cases want to build or have a reflector for your fire.

A reflector makes your fire more efficient as it radiates much of the heat back in your direction instead of just out into the environment. It also works to keep the wind from disturbing your fire. The reflector can be out of virtually anything that will last and reflect the heat back in your direction. Building a fire against a large boulder or soil bank is an excellent way to reflect the heat.

You can stack several logs on top of each other by the fire and have the fire reflect its heat.

A better way to make a reflector is to drive two stakes into the ground about a foot or so behind your fire pit, in the direction of the prevailing wind. Then pile up your fire wood supply behind these stakes. The height should be at least 3' tall. Not only will this greatly reflect the heat back toward you but it will serve the added benefit of having the smoke from the campfire climb straight up and not toward you.

People sitting around a campfire often complain that the smoke follows them around even when they move from place to place around the fire. The fact is that smoke from a campfire does follow you around! The smoke is attracted into the partial vacuum that is created by any nearby object, including you.

When you build a reflector near your fire you substitute that object as the partial vacuum. The smoke will move to that object and will then generally go straight up into the air.

When building a fire decide on the design. We have discussed the teepee fire which is good for all around purposes including warmth, boiling water, and cooking. For signaling keep some green vegetation close by so that you can toss it onto the fire to immediately create a large smoke plum that will attract rescuers.

You can build a fire surrounding it with stones. If you use stones for your fire do not gather any stones that have been in or near water. Smooth round rocks from river beds make an attractive rim for your fire but these can be deadly. Stones that have been in or around water can trap moisture inside, and when put into the fire the moisture creates steam which can result in a shattering explosion. The explosion can be severe enough to cause serious injury or even death.

Stones To Sleep With

The stones around your fire will not only serve as a wind break but they will heat up and give off heat well after the fire has died out.

To keep you warm at night, carefully remove a medium size stone from around the fire and roll it up in a piece of heavy cloth or other suitable material. Tuck the stone inside your bedding and the heat from the stone will last for hours. If your fire is burning through the night and you get cold, simply exchange that stone for another one from the fire and repeat the process.

You will be surprised at how much heat the stone gives off to keep you warm.

Fire At Night

Fires for sleeping can be made from two long logs that are positioned the length of your body. The fire will burn a long time with this much wood and you will enjoy the fire all night. In cold conditions you can build a second long log fire on the opposite side and sleep between these two fires. Be sure that the fire is far enough away that it does not catch you or your bedding on fire. In these instances it is best to use hardwoods to bank a fire for the night. Not only do the hardwoods last longer but they are much less likely to spark embers from the fire.

In some cold conditions you may need a warm place to sleep. In that case you can build a fire the length and width of your body. You can cook, boil your water and keep yourself warm until it is time to go to sleep. Then simply rake the coals away to the side, and the ground there will be very warm. When the ground cools a bit you can either sleep directly on the ground which will be very warm from the coals or put down green bedding from fir tree boughs or other foliage and you will enjoy a warm and comfortable night. The ground will continue to give off substantial heat for hours. If necessary you can use the coals to build an adjacent fire to warm you through the night.

If you have plenty of wood fuel available you may want to have two fires, one for cooking and one for a night fire that will keep you warm all night. If you are using soft wood for the night fire you will almost assuredly need to get up in the middle of the night to stoke the fire with more wood. If you stack your wood supply near you it is little effort to simply roll over and toss a few logs on the fire. The renewed crackling of the fire gives warmth and a feeling of security during a dark cold night.

Survival Stoves, What Kind Do I Need?

When looking for a survival stove to keep at home or to put into your bug-out-bag, several things need to be considered. All of these stoves have their advantages and disadvantages. You need to select a stove that meets your particular requirements. These requirements are likely to be different for a home survival situation and a wilderness survival situation.

In your home you will likely use a stove that can burn several types of fuel such as gasoline, kerosene, white gas or diesel. The versatility of these stoves allows you to not be limited to just one fuel source after a disaster. This can be a life saver in an emergency.

You are also not concerned with having a stove that is a bit heavier since this stove will primarily be used at your home in the event of a disaster. Propane stoves with the heavier metal canister are excellent stoves for home survival use.

There is nothing wrong with having more than one stove to keep at home or to pack in your bug-out-bag. You will frequently find that having two stoves is a great benefit when you want to boil water and cook your food at the same time. Having two stoves saves a lot of time.

Wood: In most survival conditions where wood is available you will probably warm yourself, cook your food and boil your water with a small wood burning stove. The nice thing about these stoves is that you can kindle a small fire with anything that you have that will burn including twigs, cardboard, charcoal, dead leaves, pine cones, bark, sap or resin chunks, animal dung, paper or anything else you have available to you. After a disaster you will likely find an enormous amount of this debris lying around.

If you are in an urban environment, particularly after a disaster hits, you can easily scrounge and find many things that are suitable to make a good wood stove and the fuel to operate it.

Advantages:

- There is no need to carry fuel. It is available for the collecting.

- A very low cost—no fuel to purchase.

- Most wood backpack stoves are lightweight and you will have no fuel to carry.

- You can easily make wood stoves out of scrap metal cans.

Disadvantages:

* You may be in areas where the only fuel you find is wet wood and it may be difficult to get a hot fire going in your stove.

* You may be in an area where wood is not available or hard to find.

* You may be in an area where wood fires are illegal.

* Wood burning stoves are notorious for creating black smudges on your cooking equipment. This is frequently transferred to the rest of your camping gear. When carrying a wood survival stove, it is always a good idea to search the area as you travel and collect small tinder and kindling that you can immediately use to start your fire when you stop to make camp.

Solid Fuel—Hexamine Fuel

These stoves are very lightweight and easy to use. These stoves use a solid "heat tab" of Hexamine fuel. One tab will generally be enough to bring a cup of water to a boil even in cold weather. The fumes from these solid fuels are toxic so they can only be used in well ventilated areas. To use, just place a tab of solid fuel in the stove and light. Set your pot on top of the stove and you are ready to cook or boil water.

Advantages of Solid Fuel Stoves:

- These are among the lightest weight stoves available on the market.

- Stoves are inexpensive to purchase—available almost anywhere.

- The fuel is very lightweight making it easy to store and pack.

Disadvantages:

* The solid fuel is generally slower for cooking time, and it is ineffective for heating up larger amounts of water to disinfect.

* Some solid fuels don't extinguish and must be completely burned after lighting, wasting fuel.

* Some of these solid fuels have a short burning time so you need to carry an ample supply with you.

Canister Stoves—Propane

Canister style stoves have become very popular because they are inexpensive, easy to carry and easy to use. These stoves use containers of propane for fuel. To use simply screw a container of propane onto the stove, turn the gas knob and light. These stoves are very fuel efficient and can bring larger quantities of water to boil.

Advantages:

* Stoves are moderately priced.

* Very clean burning with no odor.

* Screw on fuel canisters are simple to use.

* If container leaks the gas will evaporate and not harm you.

* Full simmer control.

* Propane will burn in cold weather, even at—40 Fahrenheit.

* Propane will work even at high altitudes.

Disadvantages:

* The metal fuel canisters cannot be refilled. You will need to find a place to properly discard them after use.

* Fuel for these stoves is the most expensive.

* Metal fuel canisters can be heavy to carry, particularly if you need several of them.

Canister Fuel—Butane

These are lightweight stoves that can heat up larger quantities of water. The main problem with butane stoves is that these stoves will stop working in cold weather (32 degrees F) because of the depressurization of the fuel. This can be a serious problem if you are relying on this stove in a survival situation. If you have a butane type stove and are caught in cold weather, you can try to warm the fuel by putting the container inside your coat or stuffing it inside your bedding to warm it up.

Advantages of Butane

* Stove containers are lighter than propane canisters because the butane is compressed at a lower pressure than propane. This allows the butane fuel container to have thinner walls making them much lighter.

* Small lightweight burners.

Disadvantage of Butane

* Butane does not burn well at high altitudes.

* Butane will not burn below freezing since is it not liquefied at that temperature.

Canister Blended Fuels—Butane/Propane/Isobutene

Advantages

- These stoves burn a mixture of fuels including butane, propane and isobutene fuel. They will operate at temperatures as low as 14 degrees Fahrenheit.

- Lightweight containers and small burners.

- Performs better than pure butane or isobutene in cold weather.

Disadvantages

- Fuel has a higher cost.

- At high altitudes fuel is not efficient.

White Gas Liquid Fuel Stoves

This is a cost effective stove that will operate in nearly any weather conditions. As with any stove that uses liquid fuel you need to use caution when working with these stoves. These stoves burn a liquid fuel such as white gas, aviation fuel, kerosene and gasoline. You simply pour the fuel into a metal fuel bottle, pump the stove with a built in knob to pressurize it, and then light. These stoves allow you to control the heat and flame.

These stoves are the heaviest for hikers, backpackers and those who are looking to put a stove into their bug-out-bag, but these are the only reliable stoves to use in severe cold weather.

Because of their fuel diversity, these stoves are excellent to use in urban disaster situations. You will very likely be able to scrounge fuel from automobiles, trucks, boats, storage tanks, planes or other fuel sources.

Advantages:

- Uses many different and readily available fuels found all over the world.

- Fuel is economical to purchase.

- This stove will work in extremely cold environments.

Disadvantages:

* The most expensive stove to purchase.

* These stoves have mechanical parts that will occasionally require some maintenance. In a disaster parts may not be available.

* You need to prime these stoves before lighting them. Not as easy to operate as other stoves.

* Periodically during the cooking you will need to pump the stove to maintain the needed pressure for it to burn.

Alcohol Stoves

One prime reason for having an alcohol stove is because they are simple to make and will last for years. You can build your own alcohol stove from scrap items such as tuna cans, cat food cans, and other similar metal containers. You can also purchase these at a variety of stores.

Alcohol stoves have been around for decades and have become extremely popular with hikers, backpackers and those interested in having a reliable stove for survival.

Alcohol stoves burn a variety of fuels including denatured alcohol, grain alcohol, methyl alcohol, and gelled (sterno-type) fuel. These fuels are readily available throughout the world.

These stoves are very simple to operate. Just add fuel, light and the stove is going. Most of these alcohol stoves, depending on the type of fuel you use, will boil a cup of water in less than 4 minutes, using about 3-4 teaspoons of fuel. Adding a lid to the pot will allow the water to boil faster.

Advantages:

- These lightweight stoves are inexpensive, and easy to make on your own.

- Fuel is widely available and easy to carry.

- Alcohol stoves are very easy to light. They will take any spark or match and instantly begin to burn.

Disadvantages:

* Alcohol stoves generally have lower heat output so they are not ideal when you want to heat up large quantities of water to boil.

* Alcohol stoves burn at one rate and it is hard to regulate the flame.

* Alcohol stoves are generally quite small. A larger pot on them can be unstable. You need to be careful when using the stove. If you tip the small stove over you will have hot burning fluid spilled around you.

When considering an alcohol stove consider the available fuels and the amount of energy they produce.

- Methanol: Delivers the least energy. Still useful for camping and survival situations. Has a smokeless flame.

- Ethanol: Provides a bit more energy than methanol. Useful for camping and survival situations. Has a smokeless flame.

- Isopropanol: This fuel delivers more energy than the others listed above. It provides both a cooking flame and light. This fuel does have a smoky flame that will leave a layer of soot on your pots.

Of the available fuels, 99% Isopropanol delivers the most energy.

An alcohol stove should never be used inside a tent or other confined shelter since even a blue flame produces carbon monoxide poison.

Making Your Own Tuna Can Alcohol Stove

Let's start with a very simple alcohol stove to make. There are several good things about this tiny little stove and very few disadvantages. It is extremely light weight and the fuel is relatively inexpensive. The fuel can be found all over the world. This stove is extremely easy to use.

You only need a few basic tools to make this stove. Best of all, you can make this stove in as little as 5 minutes.

Things you need:

* Empty tuna can

* Hand held paper punch (Heavy duty type is better)

* Pencil

1. Find an empty tuna can or cat food can. Any size will do.

2. Remove the label and clean the can thoroughly.

3. Use a heavy duty hand paper punch to punch a row of holes just below the top lip of the can. Space the holes about ¼" apart.

4. Now make a second row of holes below the first row. Make these holes ¼" apart and stagger them between the holes on the top row.

5. Your stove is now finished!

Use isopropanol, denatured alcohol, grain alcohol, or methyl alcohol for fuel. One of the best fuels to use is "HEET" which is a fuel line anti-freeze that is available at any automotive, hardware or variety store. Be sure to use the "HEET" product in the yellow container as the product in the red container will not work.

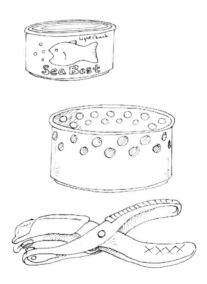

Put your stove on a flat non-combustible platform. Pour about 1/8" of fuel into the container. You do not need much fuel for this stove. Strike a match or set a spark to the fuel and it will instantly begin to burn.

You need to wait for about 20-30 seconds to allow the fuel to fully vaporize before you set your pot onto the stove. When you set your pot on the stove you will see a full "bloom" of blue flames coming out of the top row of holes in the stove. The blue flames are very hot and you will soon be boiling water on your new stove.

You will notice that your stove is extremely lightweight and will be easy to store or pack in a bug-out-bag. As mentioned earlier it is important to have more than one stove in your kit. Find another smaller tuna can or cat food can and make a second stove that neatly slips inside the first stove—two stoves in one! They take up the same space in your kit. Add a container or two of fuel in your kit and you are set.

Since these stoves are so easy to make you may want to make a couple for your home survival kit. Just keep a good supply of proper fuel on hand. Another good fuel to try is truck air brake anti-freeze (methanol). You can find this in quart size containers at most automotive stores.

Even with heavy use this little stove will last a very long time. People have used a single stove like this for years and hundreds of fires. It is very durable and will not be easily damaged. If for some reason you lose the stove or damage it, just make another one.

Making Your Own Budweiser Aluminum Bottle Stove

Another easy but more advanced alcohol stove that you can make is made from an aluminum Budweiser (long neck) beer container. It takes about 20-30 minutes to make this stove the first time. Later you will be able to make this stove in about 15 minutes or less. When finished, you will have an excellent stove that is very light weight, durable, and easy to pack. This makes an excellent alcohol survival stove.

Tools Needed:

1. One empty Budweiser-Light long neck aluminum can

2. Tool to cut bottle (knife, scissors, hacksaw, or chop saw with metal blade)

3. Sand paper to remove burrs

4. JP Weld—permanently connects pieces

5. Small file

6. Tape measure

7. ½" white tape

8. Felt ink pen

Mark around the empty bottle with a felt pen 1.5" down from the top, again at 3" down from the top (right on the curve of the bottle) and lastly at 7" down from the top.

The two pieces that you want to keep are the second and bottom section of the bottle. Throw the top piece away.

Cut the aluminum can with a sharp knife, hacksaw, scissors, bandsaw or chop saw with a metal blade. If using a knife, hacksaw or scissors, cut above the line first, and then make a finishing smooth cut with scissors on the line.

After getting the two pieces of the can, take sand paper and remove all burrs on both pieces.

When both pieces are free of burrs sit the top piece on a flat surface (neck up) and use the edge of a small file to make four 1/8" "V" notches in a crossed or "+" pattern across the top of the neck. If you do not have a file you can carefully snip these four small notches with scissors.

Now lightly fit the top piece neck down into the bottom base. Before inserting completely put some JP Weld around the top ½" of the outside of the top piece so that when you push the top piece all the way into the base, the neck with notches sits all the way down and is flush on the base of the stove. The JP Weld will keep the two pieces from separating. You may have to lay a piece of wood on top and tap on it lightly with a hammer to get the insert flush to the bottom of the stove.

When fully seated trim the top of the stove so both pieces are flush. Allow the JP Weld to set up.

Next put a piece of white tape on the top edge of the stove. Mark down about 1/2" and draw a line on the tape all around the can. Mark evenly spaced dots ¼" apart on this tape. Use a 1/16" drill bit to drill the evenly spaced holes into the **outside** wall only of the stove. Be sure that you do NOT puncture through the second inner stove wall. Remove the tape when finished.

Your stove is done! After the JP Weld has had time to properly sit, just pour some Isopropanol alcohol or other denatured alcohol into the stove (about 3-4 tablespoons) and light the fuel with a match or spark.

The alcohol will immediately begin to burn but you need to wait until the alcohol in the inner wall begins to vaporize. In about 30-40 seconds or so the stove will develop a full "bloom" in which blue flames come out all the burner holes just like the gas stove in a kitchen. You are now ready to set your pot on the stove to boil water or cook.

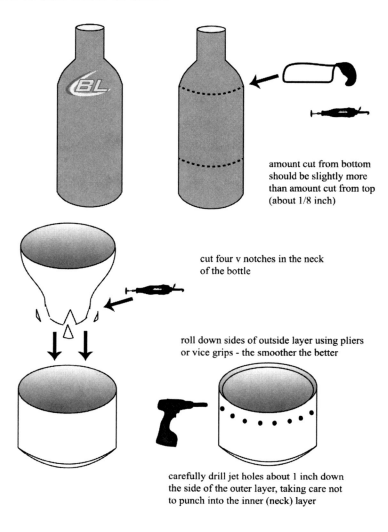

amount cut from bottom should be slightly more than amount cut from top (about 1/8 inch)

cut four v notches in the neck of the bottle

roll down sides of outside layer using pliers or vice grips - the smoother the better

carefully drill jet holes about 1 inch down the side of the outer layer, taking care not to punch into the inner (neck) layer

This stove is very efficient. The unpressurized open-top design and double wall construction enhances combustion and produces more heat than other stoves. The inner wall creates a preheat chamber that once the fuel has warmed, it vaporizes and moves up the wall to pass through the perforations to form a full fire "bloom" circle around the stove. This design improves the air to fuel mixing and increases combustion in the stove.

This simple alcohol stove can outperform some commercial stoves in cold weather where butane fuel is used.

You will be surprised at how efficient this stove can be. There are no moving parts to break and the double wall construction makes the stove very sturdy. This stove will last a long time and provide hundreds of fires. Since they are so easy to make, be sure to make several extra stoves for your home emergency supply kit, and for your bug-out-bag.

Cookware

Individuals who use the cast-iron Dutch oven have an excellent source for cooking over an open fire or on charcoals. While these pots are much too heavy to carry for backpacking, they do make a very good cookware at home in the event of a disaster. You can use this oven to cook a variety of meals in your backyard after a disaster. With proper care these ovens will last a life time.

For lighter weight cookware, both aluminum and stainless steel pots and pans are very common and make good cookware. Some are concerned that aluminum cookware may give off traces of aluminum which has been linked to Alzheimer's disease. In an emergency the occasional use of aluminum cookware should not be a major concern.

Alan Corson

Fire For Signaling

Building a signal fire is an easy and effective way to reveal your location to others. You need to prepare the correct materials for a signal fire. The signal fire must be able to produce a large amount of smoke that can be seen at long distances.

Find a good location to set your fire. You need an area that is clear of debris and flat. Try to build the fire on the highest location that you safely can. The area should be very visible from the air.

Signal fires are an excellent way to attract the attention of rescue personnel. Three separate fires set in a triangle formation is the international sign for distress.

It may be difficult to maintain three separate fires at the same time so prepare three fires but only light one for your personal needs. Be ready to immediately light the other two fires in the event you see or hear aircraft or other human activity in your area.

In daytime if you see an aircraft or hear rescue personnel in your area, you need to add green vegetation to all of your fires to create large plumes of dark smoke to mark your location. Cut green tree boughs, collect wet leaves, damp green foliage such as decayed wood or other similar materials to toss onto the fire to create a good smoke plume.

At night, fire is the most effective visual means to signal others.

When constructing signal fires in a heavy forested area you will need to find an open area that will allow others to see the fire or smoke.

If you are in a heavily snow covered area you need to clear the snow from the ground to set your fire. If the snow is too deep you need to make a platform to elevate your fire well off the ground so that the melting snow will not put your fire out.

In survival situations when your situation is dire, you can find a tree that is heavy with pitch and set that tree on fire. This can be done even if the tree is green. The pitch in the tree will easily burn creating a large fire and a huge plume of smoke. For safety reasons, try to locate a lone tree for this purpose to prevent starting a forest fire that can quickly rage out of control.

If situations merit, you can place dry wood in the lower branches of one or more lone trees and then set the kindling on fire. The kindling will quickly ignite the upper tree foliage setting the whole tree on fire. These fires and the smoke plumes they create can be seen at great distances. At night the glow from one or more burning trees illuminates brightly and can be seen for miles.

Remember to assess your particular circumstances closely to see if these extreme measures are absolutely necessary. If you start a forest fire, grassland fire, or range fire you may be held criminally and or civilly responsible for any damage it causes.

If you are fortunate enough to be in a forested area that is being monitored by personnel in lookout towers for forest fire, or from forest service observation planes/helicopters, any smoke from your fire during day time will very likely bring people to your area.

In any survival circumstances it is important that you continue to assess your circumstances and the environment that you are in. It is important that you make good decisions for your survival as events unfold around you. Think carefully about the decisions you make. Decide the best and safest course of action to help you survive.

To Go or Stay

If you are lost and the weather conditions are harsh making travel difficult, it may be preferable to stay where you are and set up good visual aids that will allow others to find you. This is particularly important when you are lost and do not know your directions. You have a better chance of walking in the wrong direction exhausting yourself and putting your life at further risk than getting it right and walking to safety. Exhaustion can be deadly in a survival situation.

In cases where you may be on a stranded train in remote snow covered mountains, or with an aircraft that has gone down in rugged territory, you want to get a clear understanding of where you are, the direction and distance that you would need to travel to reach safety.

You may be in the mountains and able to look a distance to see a road or other indication of human activity. Pay close attention to the terrain and distance that you will need to travel to get there. All too often what you can see at a distance, and what appears to be easy to reach, is far more difficult once you actually begin your travel through rough terrain. You can easily get lost in heavy timber and never reach your destination.

In cases with stranded trains and downed aircraft other people will soon realize an emergency has occurred, and rescue personnel will be on their way. You probably do not want to leave that area unless you are sure that you can reach safety a short distance away. It is much easier for rescue personnel to locate a stranded train or downed aircraft than it is for them to find a person wandering around in rugged terrain away from the scene.

Most aircraft are equipped with an emergency transponder that automatically activates should that aircraft ever crash. The transponder sends an emergency signal via satellite which immediately alerts aviation authorities of the emergency. Aircraft are also tracked on radar and their disappearance will immediately be known. Satellites provide GPS coordinates so the searchers know where the downed aircraft is located. Trains also have scheduled check points and advanced communications designed to notify others in the event of any emergency. In most cases it is preferable to stay at the scene rather than journey out on your own.

If you are stranded in a remote area in a non-commercial vehicle such as your personal car or pickup, you may not be missed by others for quite some time. There are countless stories of individuals who have taken a day trip in their vehicle into the mountains, ended up on a snow covered remote road, became stranded and died there because others did not realize that they were missing until it was too late. These individuals were not prepared to venture into that environment, and they did not have the skills to survive there.

If you are stranded in a vehicle in an emergency you have many things available to you to use. Take the spare tire and place it in a good open location and then deflate it. Build a fire on top of the tire and it will soon ignite the rubber which will produce a thick black smoke plume. The tire will burn for hours (and you have four other tires available to use if the emergency continues).

You can also cut out the contents of the vehicle's seats and put that material on your fire. Rubber car or pickup mats will burn and produce a thick black smoke. Other materials from a vehicle can be salvaged and burned to create signal smoke.

If you do not have basic survival equipment in the vehicle you can use wires from the engine and the vehicle battery to create sparks to start your tinder on fire.

At night if you hear the sound of aircraft or others in the area you can use the vehicle's headlights and horn to signal for help.

Signal smoke in a desert environment can be seen at great distances from the air. These signals are most effective when the weather is calm and the smoke hangs in the air near your location. High winds, snow storms, low clouds and rain can disperse the smoke from your emergency fire, and make it difficult for others to find your location.

Mirrors, Bright Shiny Objects, and other Visual Signals

To signal for assistance on a sunny day the best device to use is a mirror. A vehicle has several mirrors that you can use in an emergency. If you do not have a mirror with you improvise and polish any bright object that will reflect the sun's rays. You can even use the bottom of an aluminum can to catch the glint of the sun to signal your location. Under the right conditions these flashes of light can be seen a long distance away.

You can use a flashlight to signal your location. This is especially effective at night where your light can be seen a great distance from the air or from the ground.

If you have any colorful clothing or tarp you can spread that out on the ground or in a tree making it highly visible to mark your location.

SOS—Signal

If you are in a snow covered area, find a clear location that offers good visibility to the sky. Stomp the snow down to form large letters "SOS" to mark your location. You can also use large branches or logs to form this emergency signal.

In areas where you have bare soil dig out large "SOS" letters in the ground to mark your position.

You probably will not learn Morse code but you should learn the Morse code for the letters "SOS" as this is what you will most likely be using in a survival situation when you want to signal your location.

The "SOS" signal is simply three dots, three dashes and then three dots. This is the internationally recognized distress signal. A "Dot" is a short, sharp pulse such as a quick flash of light from your flashlight. A "Dash" is simply a longer pulse or longer flash of light from your flashlight.

When signaling keep repeating this "SOS" signal in the direction you want it to be seen.

Whistles

Whistles provide a very good method of signaling. Using a manufactured whistle will be heard much farther than the human voice. These are very inexpensive to purchase and easy to pack in your kit.

FOOD

Your need for food is dependent on your survival situation. People can survive for weeks without food but the accumulated detrimental effects of going without food for extended periods of time can weaken a person and hinder their ability to obtain food.

Food provides the necessary elements to stay healthy and strong.

Going without food for a prolonged time (5-7 days) will not kill the normally healthy person but it will have the effect of weakening the natural immune system subjecting the person to other conditions that will further harm the body.

A person who goes without food for 5-7 days will begin to feel the effects of the body not being nourished. The person will feel great hunger, they will become tired easily, their movements will be labored and the person's body will slowly fall into a weakened state. The longer you go without food the more progressive these effects will be.

In a short term survival situation food is not your most pressing need. However, in any survival situation you need to immediately begin thinking about rationing the food that you have and getting other food in time. Don't wait until you are nearly out of food to begin this process. You also must carefully consider the particular needs of everyone you are with.

Urban Food Storage For Disaster

In preparation for any urban natural disaster you know that you are likely to lose electricity and water for days or even weeks. Proper preparation will greatly enhance your ability to deal with the loss of basic utilities during that time.

In preparation of your survival food, collect the canned foods that your family normally uses. Keep that food supply separate to use in any disaster situation. You need to rotate that food and use it up before any expiration dates.

It is a good idea to use a felt pen to clearly mark the expiration dates on this food. That makes it much easier to review and replenish those food items with fresh food when necessary. As you prepare your disaster food supply be sure to take into account any special dietary needs of any family members.

It is best to collect and store foods with high calories and nutrition. Store food that does not require refrigeration, special preparation or water to prepare.

Be sure that you have a means to open the canned goods. A good manual hand can opener or a simple **P38 military type** key ring opener should be included with your survival food.

If your water supply is limited avoid foods high in protein, salt and fat. These foods will make you thirsty. Eat canned foods that have high liquid content.

Use perishable foods from your garden, pantry and refrigerator first.

When the power goes off and you do not have a generator, use the food in the freezer first as it will soon thaw out and begin to spoil. Limit the number of times you open the freezer door because even a well insulated freezer will only keep food for 2-3 days depending on the weather.

Always use non-perishable foods last.

Gathering Food In The Wild

Gathering food in a survival situation away from an urban environment requires different skills and a certain amount of luck. You should carefully assess your environment to determine what food sources are available to you.

Meat

When considering the types of food that you can obtain in the wild, it is important to know that a person can survive for months eating nothing more than just meat. Having a source of fresh meat, including fat from this meat, will sustain you in a survival situation for a very long time. Meat should be your primary source of food in a survival situation.

Although we may avoid this in our normal diet, eating fat in the meat is important in your survival diet since it contains about twice the calories as does protein or carbohydrates. You also want to add some fat to your diet to avoid diarrhea, which will weaken you. This is particularly the case when eating rabbit which is very lean. A steady diet of rabbit meat alone may result in diarrhea.

In a survival situation you will soon learn to disregard your socialized preferences for tastes that you have been accustomed to. Hunger will always bring a person to this point in a survival situation. Things that are edible are to be eaten. Knowing and accepting this will allow you to survive. No source of food should be discarded. The wilderness is full of natural foods that are available to you. You just have to get use to eating them.

In a survival situation there are many rules that simply do not apply. You need to eat to survive. However, some basic rules do apply. When getting meat in the wilderness you need to cook that meat to kill any parasites or bacteria that it may have. Eating raw meat may get you by for a period of time but you will likely end up regretting not taking the time to build a fire and cook that meat. The same applies to fish.

In a survival case you must know how to properly prepare and cook game and plants. If you do not properly process game it will spoil and you will not be able to eat it.

Survival Fishing

In a survival situation you need to try any available means to catch fish. Catching this food is necessary to survive. A sufficient supply of fish will go a long way in fulfilling your survival diet.

There are several ways to catch fish to eat. They can be hooked, speared, netted, clubbed, stunned, or even grabbed with your bare hands on occasion. (if you are in the right location and if you are very lucky . . .)

The best way to catch fish is with some simple commercial fishing equipment including fishing **hooks, line and weights** from your home emergency supplies or in your bug-out-bag. While it is possible to fabricate various fishing hooks in the wilderness from bones and small pieces of hardwood, it is much better to spend that precious time with your baited hook and line in the water catching fish.

If you have the necessary equipment to fish then just look around for the types of bait that fish typically eat in that area. Look under logs, in wet leaves and around flat objects and under rocks to locate worms, grubs and insects that may be used for bait. Keep in mind that these are also things that are edible for you. (more on this later)

If you can trap minnows in a small pool you can carefully hook a minnow by passing the hook through the body and under the backbone so that it does not kill the bait. When cast into the water the minnow will flail around attracting the attention of larger fish.

When you catch a larger fish make sure you save the eyes as these make good bait. Also try using small cut pieces of silver belly from a fish. The fish scales and silver meat will reflect light in the water and attract fish.

While you are scrounging for fish bait do not overlook the opportunity to find and take crawfish to eat. These are fairly simple to catch, and when you get a large handful they make a wonderful meal after being boiled in water. Crack open the shell and suck out the tender juicy morsels of meat.

Snagging

A large three point treble hook works well to catch fish, and you don't need bait. Just cast the line out and then quickly yank the line back attempting to snag any fish nearby. This works well in areas where fish have congregated in pools of water. This method is especially effective for salmon that move upstream to spawn and frequently lay in large numbers in shallow pools.

Snagging is so effective that it is illegal in most countries so you only want to use this method in a true survival situation.

Wilderness Fishing Hooks

If you do not have fishing hooks you can improvise to make wilderness hooks that will catch fish. You can use a very small piece of hardwood that is forked and carve it into a small sharp hook. Sharpen one end and tie your line onto the other. Bait the hook using natural bugs, worms and insects found in the area.

You can sharpen a small 1"-3" (depending on the size of fish) piece of hardwood tapering from the center out to form two sharp ends. Notch the center of the stick and then tie the line to this fabricated hook. Bait the hook on both ends. When the fish swallows the bait, pull the line and the stick becomes lodged in the gills, and the fish cannot spit it out.

Use small splinters of sharp bone that can be carved or ground into a sharp point using a knife or a stone. Wrap the needle bone to a small piece of wood and tie your line to the opposite end. The bone will serve as the hook.

You can improvise and use a wide variety of items to fabricate a hook. Use a small nail and grind down the tip to make a sharp point. Bend the nail into a hook shape, and then tie the line to the nail head.

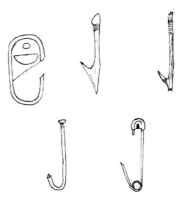

Safety pins, small pieces of wire and other items can be fashioned into hooks that can catch fish.

Make a lure to catch fish. Any small and bright piece of metal will attract fish as it flashes in the water. A tiny piece of a discarded aluminum soft drink can makes a good flasher that can attract fish to your hook. Use your knife or scissors to cut a small curved piece of the aluminum and punch a tiny hole in it so it can be attached near your hook. Use small pieces of feathers to attach to your fabricated hook to attract the attention of fish. A small piece of bright colored clothing, twine, a bit of tarp, a tiny scrap of brightly colored nylon and other similar items can be crafted into an effective lure.

You can make a float that will hold your bait off the bottom to catch fish. Take a piece of wood or other small item that floats and secure it to your line a distance from your hook. This is best used in ponds, lakes and other calm water since any water current will wash the float and bait back to shore.

You can make a weight for your line to put near your hook and that will hold the hook/bait up from the bottom.

A simple spear can be fashioned to spear fish that have congregated in a shallow pool. The spear tip needs to be very small, strong and have several sharp points. Small pieces of hardwood can be whittled into sharp points that can be lashed to the spear shaft. You can use nails and grind their tips to a sharp point on a stone. It is best to also fashion a barb on the spear to prevent fish from slipping off after being speared. Spear barbs can be fashioned from many items such as small pieces of hardwood that have been sharpened to a point and tied at an angle to the spear near the point. You can also use small slivers of bone, nails, pins, thorns from plants, and other similar materials.

If using small pieces of hard wood, harden the sharpened points of the spear in your campfire.

When spearing fish you want to correct for the refraction in the water and aim lower than where the fish appears to be in the water. It is best to have the tip of the spear in the water as you slowly close the distance to the fish. With practice you may be able to get quite close to the fish before thrusting your spear. A very slow stealthy approach is best. In some circumstances you can improvise and use small leafy limbs on your body to help camouflage your silhouette as you slowly make your approach in the water.

Use a fashioned wooden club to try to stun fish as they swim past in shallow water. At times when fish are feeding on the surface for insects you may be able to swing a large club and hit the fish that are swimming past. This may only momentarily stun the fish but you may have time to quickly catch the fish by hand and throw it onto land.

Trapping Fish

Depending on the water source, you may be able to improvise and lay rocks across a creek or stream to make a crude dam. The water will pass through the rocks but the fish cannot. Move a distance upstream and then get into the water and use a stick to splash and make considerable noise in the water as you move toward the dam.

Use your stick to splash around boulders, under ledges, and other hiding places forcing the fish to swim toward the dam. When you get near your dam build a second blocking dam behind you which traps the fish. You can then move into the pool and use a spear, club or snagging equipment to capture your meal. If you are successful be sure to remove part of both dams to allow other fish to move through and then be ready to repeat the process as necessary. When moving away from the area make sure that you open up the blockade to allow fish to move freely.

Another method to use is to make a fish trap by placing stakes and brush into the bed of the stream. Form the sticks into a "V" that allows water to pass through but the fish cannot. Again thrash about upstream forcing the fish into the trap. If the trap is well made, fish will occasionally stay in these pens for days since they are able to get food from the flowing water.

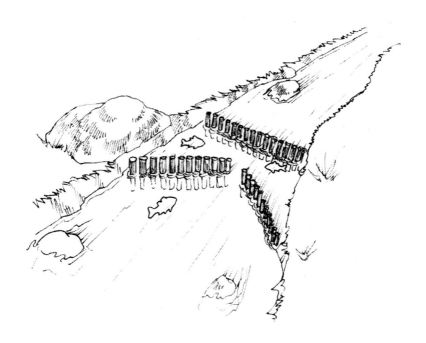

Rotenone—Killing fish

Another survival method of fishing is the use of a commercial chemical called "Rotenone." This is a chemical found in certain types of tropical plants. In the tropics the natives press certain rain forest plants from the Fabaceae family of legumes to squeeze out the juices. They introduce the plant juice into streams and lakes to kill the fish. Rotenone acts to interrupt the respiratory process in the fish killing them or causing them to surface where they are then easy to catch. The natives then gather the fish to eat. This method provided a large supply of fish for their diet. The chemical they produced was Rotenone.

Rotenone acts to kill the fish by chemically removing the oxygen in the water that fish need to breathe. It simply prevents the metabolism of oxygen by the fish.

In a survival situation, if you have just an ounce of Rotenone you can mix the liquid into a stream or creek that is 25 feet wide, and it will kill all of the fish downstream for a quarter of a mile.

Depending on the temperature of the water you will see the results in as little as 2-3 minutes but up to an hour or so in cold water. The fish will float to the surface and will eventually die. You can catch these fish by hand and cook them without any adverse effects from the poison since the fish die from a lack of oxygen. This is an excellent way to catch a large quantity of fish to eat and then smoke for later use.

Carrying even a small amount of Rotenone in your kit could furnish you with a huge amount of fish to eat and smoke.

In using this method it is best if you first move downstream and make some sort of barrier that will not allow dead fish to float past. You can use brush to block the stream or creek so that your fish will not be wasted.

After putting the liquid Rotenone into the water, wait a bit and then begin working your way downstream picking up all of the dead fish that you can find. The fish will float to the surface where they will be easy to pick up. Some fish will appear to be stunned and will swim awkwardly or they will sink to the bottom. Be sure to diligently collect every fish that you can find that has been killed by this chemical. Every fish is important to your survival and you do not want to waste any of this precious food. Eat what you need and smoke all of the rest. Do not let any go to waste.

When using Rotenone you need to know that it acts very quickly in warm water. It works much slower in colder water. It is not effective when the water temperature gets below about 50 degrees. You can use Rotenone in any small stream, creek, pond, pool or lake. You need to mix the chemical into the water to get it to work. The powder type Rotenone is not effective when sprinkled on top of the water and does not mix that well so it is best to use the liquid.

In a pinch if you have access to common lime and you throw the lime into small ponds or pools of water it will kill all the fish close to where the lime was introduced. The lime is not harmful to you in small concentrations, and you can eat the fish after proper cooking.

Some of these techniques are illegal in most areas so you only want to use them if you are in a true life and death survival situation.

Rotenone may also be used in a powdered form to treat scabies and head lice in humans. It is also sold as an organic pesticide and used in gardens to control a variety of common garden insects.

Survival Fishing—Lines In The Water

When survival fishing, you need to have as many baited hooks in the water as possible to increase your chance of catching fish.

One method is to take a length of line and tie on several stringer lines with baited hooks. The stringer lines should be at different lengths to cover as much area in the water where fish may be located. Find a good location along the bank that offers deep water. Tie an anchor such as a small stone to the end of the line and cast the line out into deep water. Allow the line to set and then tie your end of the line onto a rock, branch or other object on the bank that is strong enough to hold if several fish are caught.

This system is effective both during the day and at night. Be sure to check your set often to remove any fish that are caught and put fresh bait on the hook.

If you are in an area that has lots of trees near the river bank you can pull back an overhanging branch, tie on a line with hook. Bait the hook and release the limb allowing it to swing back out into deep water. When a fish is caught the tree limb operates like a fishing pole flexing as the fish pulls on the line keeping the line from breaking.

You can make the hook float on the surface or improvise a weight and make the hook sink into the water. You can make many of these sets along a stretch of water. Check these sets often to insure that you still have bait on your hook. These are easy to use and once made they will work day and night until you remove them.

One thing to consider is that you may want to hide your fishing lines to keep others who may walk past from seeing your fishing rig and taking any fish that you have caught as well as your line and hooks. With the line containing multiple stringer lines and hooks, this can be done by positioning your end of the line over and down the bank where it is not easily seen by someone walking past. Push a small bush into the bank to hide where you have secured the line.

To hide the tree limb fishing lines try to pick a branch that overhangs the water in such a way that it will naturally hide your line so that it is not easily seen by a person walking past.

Frequently you will have natural game trails that follow near water sources. Sometimes people will follow these trails (the easiest path) looking for game or a place to fish. One good method to keep strangers from getting too close and spotting your fishing rig is to put up natural obstacles that will guide a person away from your fishing line and then allow them to naturally guide back to the bank of the river where they are wanting to walk. You can use simple objects such as thorny brush, branches, tree limbs, or other natural objects to discretely discourage people from walking close to your set. These objects need to appear natural and not something that you have constructed to hide something. People will walk around these obstacles, taking the easiest path, and then work their way back to the trail never knowing your fishing set is there.

It may also be useful for you to use a leafy branch to lightly brush out any tracks on the trails in several locations near your camp or your fishing area. You can then revisit these areas to see if there has been any human or game activity on those paths. It is always a good idea to know what is happening in your area, and if any of this activity puts you in danger.

Preparing Fish To Eat

All fish in North America are edible. Most saltwater fish can be eaten although there are a few varieties that are poisonous. Almost all of the poisonous fish are found in the tropics. Many of these poisonous fish can be recognized by their hard skins, or when their bodies are protected by spines or plates. When out a distance at sea most of the salt water fish are good to eat. When you begin getting close to shore you may encounter some saltwater fish that are not edible.

When you catch a fish you need to immediately gut and clean the fish so that it does not spoil. Cooking freshwater and salt water fish effectively kills any parasites and bacteria they may have. Some saltwater fish can be eaten raw as the salt water helps to eliminate parasites but the safe practice is to always cook the fish before eating.

Use your knife to cut off the gills and gut the fish cleaning out the gut cavity. Save the guts of the fish and use it as bait for fishing or trapping. Check the stomach to see what the fish are eating. Use that same bait if you can. Use the food in the fish stomach for your next bait.

A fish will spoil quickly in hot weather so prepare the fish for eating as soon as possible. If you catch a fish and want to continue fishing it is a good idea to put a line or a forked branch through the gills and let the fish stay in the cool shaded water until you are finished fishing.

Be sure that you do not eat fish that appears to be spoiled. Even if you cook the fish it will not ensure that the spoiled fish will be edible. Eating spoiled fish can make you sick. You may get diarrhea, vomit or become nauseated.

When cooking your fish over a fire use hardwoods if possible rather than soft woods which contain resin or sap. Fires with softwoods will tend to tarnish the taste of the fish. When you are using coals to cook your fish the hardwoods also burn much slower and the embers are better for cooking.

To cook your fish you can simply impale a whole fish on a sharp green stick and cook it over an open fire. Rotate the fish occasionally to cook the fish on all sides. You can also wrap the fish up in wet green leaves and place it onto campfire coals to cook. Turn occasionally to cook both sides evenly.

To get the most nutrients from your fish you should boil the fish in a pot with the skin on. The oils and fat in the skin provide excellent nutrition and the juice broth is healthy for you.

You can also fillet a fish, which is simply cutting the fleshy sides of the fish away from the carcass. You can cook these slabs of meat over the fire, fry in a pan or smoke them for later use. Smaller fish (less than 8") do not need to be scaled and can be cooked by roasting over the fire or fried in the pan. For small fish leave the head and tail on to keep the fish intact while cooking.

If you have a larger fish you may want to scrape off the scales before cooking. To do this simply lay the fish on a rock or other suitable object and use your knife blade to scrape off the scales. It is best to hold the fish by the tail and work your blade toward the head of the fish.

If you have caught more fish than you need for one meal, smoke the fish for later use. It is always a good idea to have your wilderness smoker prepared, the wood racks built, and your wood ready so you can quickly begin smoking the fish when you return to camp. You certainly do not want to have your fish spoil while you are making your smoke tent.

Smoking Meat

To smoke your fish (or any other meat that you have) you need to build a small fire and partially enclose the fire so the meat is exposed to the smoke. You can use the **tarp shelter** in your bug-out-bag for this. You want the fire to produce smoke and not heat. Use hardwoods for your fire because soft wood that is resinous will ruin your meat. The wood should be somewhat green so that it burns but creates a nice smoke on the fire. You will probably want to start your fire with dry wood and when it burns down add semi-green limbs to get a nice smoke going for the meat.

Take the meat and cut it into thin slices. Place the meat on an improvised wood framework that is placed close to the fire but far enough away that it does not catch on fire or burn the meat. Keep the meat pieces separated. Do not stack slices of meat on top of each other. You want the smoke to reach all areas of each piece of meat.

Wrap the tarp around the meat as much as possible to allow the fire to continue to burn but also hold the smoke. Occasionally add small bits of fuel to the fire to keep the smoke going. Keep the fire burning low so that it does not get too hot and burn the tarp or meat.

The Family Guide to Survival. Skills that Can Save Your Life and the Lives of Your Family

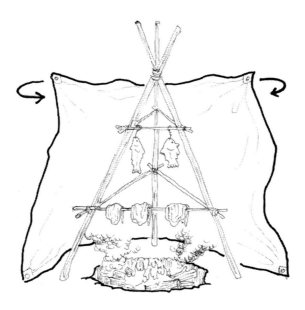

Keep the meat in your improvised smoker all day. If at all possible leave the meat in the smoker for two days. Meat smoked in this manner will last for about 1-2 weeks.

Pit Smoking Fish

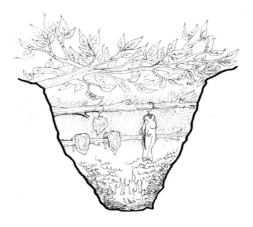

You can also smoke meat in a pit. Dig a pit large enough to accommodate the wooden racks that hold the strips of meat. Put a base down and then build a fire in the pit. Add semi-green wood to get a good smoke from the fire. After the fire has burned down some, lay a heavy layer of brush across the pit or cover the pit with logs to hold the smoke inside but still allow the fire to get oxygen to burn. Continue feeding the fire occasionally so it continues to smoke the meat.

After smoking you can eat saltwater fish without any further cooking. With freshwater fish, you need to cook the meat to eliminate any parasites it may contain. Again, it is always best to cook either saltwater fish or freshwater fish before eating to insure that it does not have any parasites.

Sun Drying Fish

Fish can also be preserved by drying the meat in the sun. Select a sunny spot and hang the fillets of fish from branches or makeshift wood racks. They can also be dried by laying them on large flat rocks that are exposed to the sun.

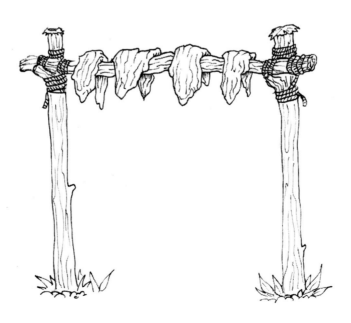

After the meat is dried add a bit of salt to help cure it. If you do not have salt you can add a splash of saltwater instead. You need to be sure that the meat is completely dried. Be sure to cook the meat before eating.

Freezing Meat

If you are in a cold climate you can freeze meat and it will keep indefinitely. Frozen meat when thawed still needs to be cooked because freezing does not kill any parasites or bacteria.

Snake . . . The Other Meat

Snake meat is included in this book not because it tastes good but because it is a meat that can be found almost everywhere in the world and it is relatively easy to catch.

Snakes can be a valuable source of meat. Never pass up a chance to add this to your survival diet. Just don't expect this to taste like gourmet restaurant meat covered in a nice white sauce. You will also have to spend considerable time picking out the bones before eating.

Snakes can make for an easy survival meal because they can be found almost everywhere but you need to exercise some caution when adding snake to your survival diet. Some snakes are poisonous and can make you very sick or kill you. Even non-poisonous snakes can leave a nasty bite that can be painful and the bite area may get infected.

The best way to capture a snake is by using a straight stick about 5-6 feet in length preferably with a small fork at the end. When you locate a snake use the stick to trap the snake's head by pinning it to the ground. This allows you to control the snake and safely cut off the head with a knife. After the head is cut off be sure that you do not touch the head as the snake's venom can still harm you if you somehow poke yourself with the fangs. Carefully handle the head with sticks or other suitable object, and bury it well away from your location.

Next, skin the snake by taking your smaller knife and enter the snake skin at the anus near the tail. Slide the knife blade up just under the skin toward where the head was located (now removed).

Peel the skin off the snake beginning near the top. You may find quite a bit of connective tissue so you want to work your knife between the skin and carcass. Cut through the connecting fibers and muscles. Work your way all around the snake pulling on the skin down as you go. Continue this until you have skinned a few inches down from where the head was located. Once you have enough skin to grab, just pull to peel the skin down the body of the snake.

After skinning the snake you need to remove the guts. Do this by grabbing the guts and pulling. The guts are in a tube along the snake's body and will rip out easily.

Wash the snake meat and clean it carefully.

Cut the snake into pieces and boil it for a stew or add to other edibles in the pot. Cook the snake meat in the same manner as other small game. For a quick meal place a piece of meat on a sharp green stick and roast it over the fire. Enjoy!

Trapping Game. There are several good techniques to trap wild game.

Deadfall Trap

This is a simple technique that kills the animal when the bait is hit and a weight falls onto the animal. This trap can be made to fit the size of the animal you are hunting.

Trigger

An often-shown trap is one carved from a small branch. It's very effective but you will likely need practice to make it work well. Without practice making and setting this trap it will be difficult to trap your animal. You want to make the trap stable but collapse at the slightest disturbance of the bait.

A stick is set in a horizontal position and bait bar is balanced at appropriate angles to an upright stick. Use a heavy flat rock or a log for weight.

Another variation of the trigger mechanism is also made from sticks. This is easier to make and no tools are required. Just use two long sticks and one short stick made with proper cuts to make it work.

Where To Put The Trap

Before setting your traps look closely around the area. You need to decide where to set the trap that is most likely to catch game. Look for game trails and any natural bottleneck on a path where you can place a trap. Put your trap where animals appear to have recently traveled. Try to set the trap quickly and leave the area before you leave too much human scent. Animals tend to avoid areas of human scent.

When trapping for game you need to set as many traps as you can to enhance your chances of catching game. Check your traps often. You want to quickly remove any game caught in your trap. Reset the trap and then proceed with skinning, processing and cooking the game to eat.

It is much better to try trapping small game and birds than to set your goal on larger animals like deer or elk.

As in any survival preparation, you need to practice these skills before a disaster happens. Only then will you know that you are proficient with these survival skills. Remember, these skills take time, patience and practice.

Snaring Game. Snaring game is a simple and effective means of getting meat. It requires less skill than hunting and can require much less energy to get your food.

A person prepared for wilderness survival should have several small game snares or a spool of snare wire as part of their kit. If you do not have commercial snares or snare wire, making simple snares that are effective on small animals and birds can be accomplished with fishing line, twine, small rope or other small cordage.

When making the snare make sure that the noose is large enough to go over the animal's head but not so large that the animal can step through the noose. You want to set the snare at about the animal's chest so that when the animal is walking naturally it will pass its head through the noose. You need to support the snare with branches and other material that will camouflage the noose and wire and hold the snare at the right height. It is also important to securely anchor the snare to prevent the animal from running off after it is snared.

Snares are very effective for small game such as rabbits and squirrels.

Practice these survival skills, not because you need them today, but because one day your life may depend on them.

In any survival situation the time and energy that you spend must be productive to your survival goals. It makes little sense to burn up more calories trying to catch game than the calories that you get from the animal. This is why snares are such an important tool to have in a survival situation.

Making and setting snares takes a minimum amount of time, energy or equipment. You can set several snares and then go about other chores while the snares are working for you. Snares are very reliable and effective ways to get the meat that you need to survive. Snares work all day, all night, and in any weather to catch game. When game is caught you simply remove the animal, reset the snare and continue with your other survival priorities.

In survival situations you will most likely be snaring small game such as rabbits, squirrels, chipmunks and other small animals. You will have the best success snaring these small animals.

You must build and set your snare for the specific type of animal you are attempting to catch. A snare set for a squirrel will not work for a rabbit size animal.

To effectively use a snare you must carefully select the place to set the snare. It does little good to set a bunch of snares out hoping that something will be caught. Snares must be placed in those areas where small animals frequently travel.

Good places for snares are on small game trails that have signs of recent use. Look for fresh tracks, animal droppings, scrapes, disturbed vegetation where animals have eaten, nesting or roosting areas, and other signs of recent animal activity on the trail.

Look for paths near water sources as animals will frequently use these small paths daily to get water, hunt for food and return to their den or bedding area.

When selecting a location to set a snare on a game trail, look for areas where the trail naturally narrows. Look for areas where the animal needs to walk through a narrow area on the trail.

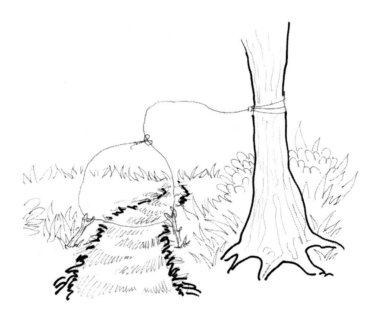

You will frequently find a small animal trail in very thick brush. Animals will almost always use these trails since the adjacent area is so thick and difficult to move through. These are very good areas to set snares.

You can set a snare in this thick brush by placing a strong stick over the trail on top of the heavy brush. Tie the snare wire to this stick and then set the loop over the trail at the proper height for the animal you are after. Be sure that the loop is up off the ground enough so that the animal cannot step through the loop.

When the animal walks through placing its head into the noose and pulls, the noose will close and the stick will be pulled down into the heavy brush. When the animal pulls, the stick will get caught in the thick brush and the noose will kill the animal.

You can also fabricate a natural funnel to make the animals walk on the trail where you have set the snare. Animals by nature live their lives conserving their energy. Animals, if not under any stress or anxiety will usually take the path of least resistance if given the opportunity. This means animals will generally walk in areas that allow them to move without having to push through brush or jump over objects when they have the opportunity to simply walk around them. You can use this to make the animal walk in the area where you have set your snare.

This can be done by placing the snare on a game trail using natural objects such as trees, large rocks, stumps, banks of soil or other natural objects that are found on one side of the trail. Place other natural objects such as a few pieces of brush, small branches, sticks or other natural objects that cause the animal to walk around those objects and "funnel" into your snare. These funneling objects must appear natural or the animal may shy away from that area. You want the "funnel" on the trail to be an area that is just a bit wider than the body of the animal that you are targeting. The "funnel" does not have to be an impossible barrier but simply moving through the funnel will be the easiest route for the animal to take.

When looking for a place to set a snare look for signs of animal dens, burrows or freshly dug holes in the ground. The soil around these entrances will indicate if recent activity has occurred. If the soil appears to have been recently disturbed set a snare there and you will likely catch an animal.

For survival purposes you do not need to learn the hundreds of different methods to make and set snares. You just need to have a good working knowledge on how to set a proper snare that has a high success rate for catching game. Many of the snare designs follow the same basic snaring principals.

It is best to prepare all of your snares at camp and then take them out to be set. When you set any snare or trap you leave human scent at that location. Animals have learned to avoid humans, and if you linger near a set too long animals will shy away from that area and your snare will not catch any game.

It is important to mask your scent at any snare set. Animals have a keen sense of smell and leaving your scent on the small wire may be just enough to alarm the prey and make it avoid your snare.

With a bit of preparation you can remove your scent from the snare by using natural materials you find. Use a handful of rotten leaves or fresh vegetation to wipe down the snare wire before setting it. Animal dung, wet rotten wood, tree leaves, pine, cedar or fir needles or a bit of charcoal from your last camp fire can be used to masks your scent by wiping the snare wire as you make the set. Animals are very familiar with these smells and accept them in their environment. One benefit of sitting around a campfire is that your clothes will absorb some campfire smoke. This will help reduce your human scent at your sets. You can also rub your hands in the cold ashes of a campfire to help eliminate the scent on your hands before you set the wire snare.

Sometimes in setting the snare you will disturb the ground where the snare has been set. Freshly scraped soil will appear unnatural to many animals and they will be on alert and possibly shy away from that area and your snare. Be sure that you toss some leaves or other debris around to make the area look as natural as possible before you leave your set. Use a tree limb to brush out your footprints and other indications that you were there.

If the snare sits in the weather for a day or so that will also effectively reduce the human scent from the snare and area.

When making the set try to use a bit of natural camouflage from leaves and vegetation to hide the presence of the snare wire. The object is to make the area look as natural as possible while at the same time causing the animal to enter your snare.

Material To Make A Snare

1. Galvanized Cable

The best snaring material for small game is 1/16" galvanized aircraft cable. This is light weight, very strong, water resistant, easy to use and takes very little space. Commercial snares have a small locking mechanism that prevents the snare from loosening after the animal is caught. This device can then be manually released so the snare can be reset.

Most trappers use this as their primary snare set up. This cable can be purchased at most hardware stores or snare/trapping shops.

It is important that you do not use ordinary thin holiday wire that is found at most convenience stores. This wire is simply too light and brittle for snaring purposes. You do not want to spend a lot of time and energy in a survival situation setting snares only to return to find that all of the snares have broken wire and no game. Trying to twist this holiday wire into multiple strands may work in a pinch but it will not work as well as regular snare wire, which costs about the same. If your survival depends on catching meat, you do not want cheap wire to be the reason that you went hungry.

2. Snare Wire

The second choice is snare wire. This wire should be 22 gauge, galvanized and specifically intended to be used for snares. This wire is strong enough to hold but can easily be molded into a snare loop. Each snare should be about 30" long. That gives enough length to make a proper size loop with enough wire left over to tie off to a good anchor. Snare wire is very inexpensive and you can purchase a small 100' roll that would be more than adequate for survival purposes.

If you are in a situation where you do not have commercial snares or snare wire with you, search around to find cordage that will work. The wiring from a motor vehicle, aircraft, or other vehicle will work. Small strips of wire from appliances can make good snares too. Strands of twine, string, small rope, cord, fishing line, heavy thread, or thin leather stitching can be fabricated into snare material.

If you are in the wilderness and do not have any of these items, you can use Milkweed, Cattail, Stinging Nettle, or strips of cedar or elm tree bark to craft into light cordage for snaring small animals. You can make a snare from small strips of hide taken from the animals that you have caught. Snaring has been around for hundreds of years, long before snare wire was available so it may take you some time but you will be able to fashion snares from this material. When using wilderness cordage you can shorten the length of the snare to about 20 inches.

Twitch-Up Snare

This is basically a snare that uses a green sapling that when bent over will provide enough force to activate a snare. The best wood for this is a hardwood. To make this sapling more effective, remove all of the limbs and leaves allowing it to "whip" up when triggered. A simple wooden trigger is carved to operate this snare.

Trigger Spring Snare

Parts:

* Snare Wire—Noose

* Trigger carved from wood and notched base stick

* Cordage to connect to the end of the snare wire

This snare operates when you make the noose over the trail. Connect the snare wire to a trigger, which is a piece of wood with a notch cut into it. The top of the wood trigger is connected with wire or other cordage to a bent over sapling, which provides the energy for the snare. The trigger is lightly connected in a notch in a base stick that is stuck into the ground beside the trail. The base stick lightly holds the trigger piece in place. The snare functions when the animal sticks their head through the noose tripping the trigger which causes the sapling to whip up snaring the animal.

There are many different trigger mechanisms that will work on this type of snare.

This snare system can also be used for fishing. Just modify the system to have the fishing line attached to the bottom of the trigger. When a fish takes the bait and moves the line the trigger will release causing the limb to whip up hooking the fish.

There will be many times that you may not have a convenient sapling near your game trail or where you want to fish. In those instances you may need to cut a suitable sapling and stake it in the position for your snare. You can also improvise and use a log or rock to serve as the weight to lift the snare. This is accomplished by tying the line to a heavy branch or small log and passing the line over a branch of a tree to the snare trigger. When the trigger is tripped, the weight of the branch or log falling will serve to lift and snare the animal.

Squirrel Pole

Squirrel snares are simple to make and can be quite productive. All you need is a few feet of snare wire, and a tree where squirrel activity can be seen.

Squirrels are like most animals in the wild and will take the path of least resistance to reach their destination. A convenient pole to run up a tree is much easier than having to climb the tree straight up from the ground. You can use that knowledge to snare them.

Find a long relatively straight pole and trim off most of the limbs. You will want to put several snares on this pole.

Take the snare wire and make a loop slightly larger than a squirrels head. Bend the wire so that the loop is up and off the pole at about the chest height of the squirrel. The remaining wire should be securely tied to the pole. Use the natural twigs and smaller limbs on the pole to help camouflage your snares a bit.

Lay this branch containing several snares at about a 45 degree angle against the tree. Snug the pole in firmly so that it does not move.

Squirrels are curious animals and they will eventually walk up the pole and get caught in the noose. The squirrel will fall off the pole and will be strangled. Other squirrels will not be bothered by this, and they too will walk up the pole and get caught in a wire snare.

This set up can produce several squirrels for the pot.

As with any wildlife that you catch, be sure to use all of the animal's parts. Many times the hide from rabbits can be used to make carrying pouches, hand warmers and many other useful items. Bones can be used for hooks, sewing needles, and spears. The hide can be used for making cordage for a variety of uses. Small pieces of fur from a squirrel's tails make an excellent fishing lure.

Keeping a few snares or small roll of snare wire in your kit provides you an excellent means to catch food to eat. You will also find the wire useful for many other survival tasks.

How to Prepare a Squirrel For Eating

Squirrel meat is very tender and tasty. They make an excellent meal when you catch them. After getting the squirrel you need to gut the animal and remove all of the entrails. Do this by putting the squirrel on a clean surface. Make a cut into the belly of the animal but do not pierce into the stomach. Use your fingers to enlarge the cut, opening the belly of the animal exposing and removing the guts. Keep the guts and eyes for fish bait.

The next step is to skin the squirrel. They are easy to skin particularly when they are still warm. Take your knife and make a slit across the squirrel's back about 3" up from the tail. Put your fingers of both hands inside this slit and pull apart. By pulling you will peel the skin in both directions. Continue to peel and remove all of the skin working it over the head and feet. Rinse out the body cavity and the squirrel is ready to be cooked.

Rabbits and other small game can be processed in the same manner.

Preparing Large Game

All large game is good to eat but some of the raw meat may contain parasites so you need to properly cook the meat before eating.

Large animals such as bear, deer, elk, caribou and moose are large bodied animals that may be difficult for one person to handle during the butchering process. You will need a good knife to butcher the animal.

As soon as the animal has been killed, bleed the animal by cutting its throat. Collect as much blood from the animal as you can since it is rich in vitamins and minerals. You can add it to your stew pot later.

If you are alone and unable to hoist the animal by its front legs with a rope into a tree, you can butcher the animal by positioning the animal on its back on level ground. If you need to butcher the animal on ground that is sloped, put some stones or a log on the downward side of the animal to keep it from rolling as you butcher it.

Make a cut into the hide near the anus. Hold the blade with your fingers at an angle so the blade is upwards as it cuts into the skin but does not cut into the stomach and internal organs. Slide the blade under the skin cutting up to the chest breastbone. This should open the belly to expose the internal organs without cutting into them.

Use your hatchet to cut through the breastbone toward the neck to open the chest cavity and allow access to all the internal organs and windpipe. If you do not have a hatchet you can use your heavy knife blade. Tap the blade with a piece of wood to force it through the breastbone.

Cut out the diaphragm muscles located inside the chest cavity. You can now begin to carefully remove the guts. Be sure to slowly remove the guts so that you can find and save the liver and heart as these are very good to eat. They contain lots of vitamins and minerals. Put the heart and liver on some clean surface for use later.

Be sure to carefully locate and remove the gall bladder of the animal. Do not rupture this sack of fluid as it will taint the meat.

When the guts are removed, reach inside the chest cavity and cut out the windpipe and esophagus as close to the neck as possible. These will be slick so use your knife and pull at the same time to remove them.

Now that the animal is gutted you need to remove the hide. Continue the cut near the anus toward the first joint on both of the rear legs. On the front legs cut from the first joint down toward the breastbone where your cut will meet the cut made into the belly.

Since the animal is too heavy to lift, simply cut one side of the skin to the backbone. Spread out that half of the skin and then roll the animal onto it and continue skinning the other side. Try to keep the meat as clean as possible. If you have a tarp or sheet of plastic available this helps keep the meat clean as you butcher the animal.

After skinning it is necessary to hang the meat to cool. You will probably need to cut the meat into quarters or large pieces which will be easier to handle.

You want to use every scrap of meat from the animal and let nothing go to waste.

Even the tougher neck meat can be made into shish kabobs and roasted over the fire or cut up into chunks and made into a wonderful stew. Clean every scrap of meat off the bones.

One part of the animal that is often overlooked is the tongue. Properly cooked deer, elk or caribou tongue makes a wonderful meal.

There are some concerns about eating deer due to a disorder called Chronic Wasting Disease (CWD). This disease is always fatal for the animal and is spreading in deer populations in some states in the U.S.A. This disease is similar to Mad Cow Disease (bovine spongiform encephalopathy). The disease has been around for more than 20 years. During this time many hunters have probably eaten meat from infected animals, but no cases of human CWD have yet been documented.

There are a few common sense ways to avoid this problem.

* Do not eat any animal that appears sick.

* Do not eat the brains, eyes or lymph nodes of any deer.

Edible Insects

When faced with a survival situation insects are one of the most available and nutritious food sources that are available to you. Insects are rich in protein, fat, carbohydrates and vitamins.

The very thought of eating insects may be repulsive to you but that will all change when you are in a survival situation and hunger overrides your socialized eating habits. It also may mean the difference between living and dying.

You should begin introducing insects into your diet early in any survival situation because it offers good nourishment and you do not want to wait until you are starving to begin eating these tasty little morsels.

Insects can be found in substantial quantities and they are easy to catch. Grasshoppers for example are easy to pick up from bushes and from the ground. They should be cooked before eating to kill any parasites.

Searching among dead logs and wet leaves will produce termites, an excellent source of food. Grubs and earthworms all make for excellent protein for the survival diet. These should be cleaned well and the earthworms squeezed to remove the soil from their stomachs before boiling. While some of these insects can be eaten raw, it is always better to boil them before eating.

Ants are found just about anywhere in the world. Collecting ants from their nest in the ground is the best way to get enough to eat. One simple way to collect ants is to poke a stick into the nest and agitate it a bit. When ants cling to the stick pull it out and place the stick into a container of water washing the ants off. Repeat this process until you have a good amount of ants. You can eat dead ants raw but most prefer them cooked.

You should avoid insects that are likely to carry diseases. These include ticks, mosquitoes and flies. Also avoid poisonous insects such as spiders, and scorpions. The general rule to follow is to avoid all insects that are a bright color or those fuzzy insects or insects covered with fine hair. You also want to avoid eating pungent insects and bugs.

In any survival situation always stay with the insects that you know are safe. You will find plenty of termites, grubs and worms to fill your plate without having to venture into eating insects that you are not sure of and may harm you. It is always best to study which insects are in your area and which are edible in a survival situation.

Bird Eggs. Wild bird eggs offer high nutrition and are safe to eat. Eggs can be boiled or fried. Look for bird nests in trees and occasionally you will find bird nests on the ground or in a hole.

It is important to understand that many wild bird eggs around the world are protected and collecting and eating wild bird eggs should only be done in a true survival situation.

Frogs. You can often capture frogs at night. Listen for their distinct croaking to pin point their location. You can sneak up on them and use an improvised club or use a treble hook to snag them. With practice you will be able to spear them.

At night you can use a light to shine into their eyes and capture their attention long enough for you to grab them with your hand.

Be sure to skin all frogs before cooking as the skin may be toxic. Cooked frog legs are very tasty and you can eat the whole frog.

The same is possible with salamanders where frogs are often found. Remove the scaly skin and boil, or fry them over a fire.

Steamed Clams

This is a tasty meal but it takes time to prepare. You can fix steamed clams even without a container.

Dig a pit and line the pit with hot stones from your fire. Put the clams into the stones in the pit. Cover with a bunch of wet seaweed. If you are not near the coast and do not have access to seaweed cover the clams with wet grass or wet leaves. When you have a pile covering the clams, probe a stick down through the grass or seaweed into the rocks. Pack several inches of sand or dirt over everything. Carefully remove the stick and pour in a small amount of water so that it gets to the clams through the dirt and grass/seaweed. This water on the rocks will cause the steam.

Pull the stick out and cover the hole. Allow things to cook for about 4-5 hours or so. When done, carefully dig out the clams which should be done and ready to eat.

Wild Edible Plants

Finding wild edible plants including fruits, berries and nuts is an important survival skill.

Depending on your location and the season, you will almost always find some type of edible plant. If you have the knowledge of only a few of these edible plants it will be of significant help to you in a survival situation.

In preparing for any disaster or wilderness survival, be sure to learn what plants around you are edible. This should be done well before you are suddenly put into a survival situation.

In many survival books you will be told in detail about the methods to test wild plants to see if they are edible. The end result of course is to find out if the plant can be safely eaten. This testing process can take many hours for each plant. The last step of course is to swallow a small piece of the plant and then wait for half a day or more to see if you get sick.

While nice to know, this method is best left for those who are not in either an urban or wilderness survival situation.

While there are literally thousands of plants that are edible, most people who suddenly find themselves in an urban or wilderness survival situation will not be able to distinguish those plants that are edible from those that are not. Some plants are poisonous and can kill you if you eat even a small portion.

In a survival situation you simply do not want to waste your time or energy foraging around testing pieces of plants for days to try to find something to eat.

The truth of the matter is that in a survival scenario it will be extremely difficult for a person to gather enough wild plants to get the necessary calories they need to survive. Depending on the season and environment, this may be nearly impossible to achieve. Plants alone simply do not provide the necessary calories that are needed for an active person to survive.

All too often people who are lost in the wild will become hungry after a very few hours and eventually they begin to forage on any plants that they may find to fill their bellies. While this may work for awhile, these individuals will inevitably find some good looking plant that appears to be something that they have eaten before, (like mushrooms) and after eating this plant they will become seriously ill and may die.

You can be sure that if you are in a survival situation and happen to choose to eat the wrong plant (and at some time you surely will) you will have serious problems that will compromise your ability to survive.

Eating unknown plants is dangerous. Do not take the risk of serious injury or death by eating unknown plants. Eat only the plants that you know are safe to eat.

Having given that admonishment, you need to know that plants are an excellent food source in the wild but it will be difficult to get all of the nutrition that you need from just plants. Plants can be added to your survival diet as long as you are sure of what you are eating.

Also, be sure that you do not make the mistake of watching what plants animals eat and assume the same is edible for you. Some animals thrive on poison plants such as poison ivy. Squirrels thrive on various types of poison mushrooms. You cannot rely on what animals eat and consider those plants something you can include in your diet.

You must not eat any plant in the wild unless you are absolutely sure that it is edible.

Learning some easy to recognize plants will allow you to add these plants to your diet.

Clover This plant flourishes in many parts of the world. As children we have all tasted the tiny bits of honey in this plant. You can boil up a nice cup of clover tea if you collect the full grown dry flowers, crush them in your hand and put about a teaspoon of this into a cup of boiling water. Allow the clover to steep in the same manner as ordinary tea.

Dandelion Another well known and easily recognizable plant is the dandelion. One of the most commonly found plants that is often considered a weed. Many of us have spent considerable time and energy trying to eradicate this plant from our property.

All of the dandelion plant is edible even the roots. The flower can be eaten straight from the plant. It has a mild sweet taste. The young tender leaves of the plant are the best. As they mature the older leaves will turn a little bitter. Boiling older dandelion leaves will remove some of the bitterness.

Dandelion roots are best prepared by peeling them and then slicing them. Put the peeled dandelion roots into a boiling pot of water until they are somewhat soft. The dandelion root will have a bit of bitterness that can be tamed down with a pinch of salt. The water from the boiled dandelion makes a nice tea.

You can put the whole dandelion plant into the pot of water and boil until soft and then eat.

Milkweed

Another very recognizable wild edible plant that is found all across the United States is the milkweed. This plant is commonly found in wet fields and marshes.

To cook this plant, place young leaves into a pot of boiling water and simmer until tender. The greens are quite good to eat.

Use the stalks of milkweed with the best being stalks that are about 8" in length. Cook these stalks until they are tender.

When cooking milkweed all parts of the plant are initially bitter because of the milky sap. The sap is soluble in water so you will need to bring it to a boil and then pour off the liquid a time or two to get to the taste that you can handle.

Burdock

This plant with the large prickly seed heads may appear to not be good to eat but you can actually eat the whole plant. The leaves are best boiled to reduce some bitterness in them. The plant stem can be peeled and eaten raw. The plant root can be boiled in a pot and then eaten.

Cattails

This plant is found in wet marshy areas all around the world. These plants can be eaten either raw or cooked. The plant is edible from the starchy roots to the plant spikes. This is an excellent survival food and can provide nutrition through all four seasons.

In the fall and winter you can use the large roots (rhizomes) of the plant. Just locate the cattail and pull up the roots. Separate the root from the cattail stalk by cutting the stalk off so you only have the root. Keep the stalk since there is valuable food in the corns or that part of the plant pending next year's growth. These are found either growing on the roots or near the base of the stalk. The lower part of the stem can be eaten either raw or boiled. The cattail leaves can be boiled.

Wash the roots which are likely to be covered with mud. Use any surface water nearby to wash the roots before boiling.

Remove and peel the corns with a sharp knife. These are the small shoots that are near the base of the stalk and are found on the roots. These corns can be eaten raw after being washed with disinfected water.

Collect a bunch of the greenish yellow spikes from the plant before they become loaded with pollen. Remove the outside thin sheath and put it into boiling water for a few minutes until the plant is tender.

The thick golden pollen that appears later in the season on the flower can be collected and made into a cereal by simmering in small amounts of water.

In the first foot of the plant stalk you will find the tender white part which can be eaten raw or cooked.

Dock

This plant is sometimes called "Sour Dock" or "Yellow Dock." This plant has tender young leaves that can be eaten either raw or when boiled in water briefly. The plant's stalk can be peeled and eaten raw or boiled in a pot of water. The plant's seeds (a lot of them on each plant) can be ground up into a flour to bake with.

Plantain

This is another prolific plant that can be found in a wide variety of climates and locations in the wild and in urban settings such as public parks and wetlands. The leaves of this plant can be eaten either raw or lightly boiled. The plant's seeds are also edible.

Plantain is not only a food source but it has been used to treat minor cuts and insect bites. Chew up a few leaves and then apply them to the bite or wound. This process will need to be repeated as necessary.

Purslane

This plant is another plant that we often associate as being a weed. We frequently try to get rid of this plant from our property. This low-growing plant makes a very good plant food and it can be found in many areas. The leaves of the Purslane can be eaten either raw or after boiling. The stem and seeds of the plant can also be eaten either raw or when boiled.

Shepherd's Purse

This plant is another good food source for survival. It can be found in many of the same areas where you find dandelion and purslane. Pick the young leaves and eat them raw or after boiling lightly. The older leaves from this plant can be boiled much like dandelions to remove some of the bitter taste. Search the pods of this plant and locate the seed which is also edible.

Lamb's Quarters

This plant is also called "goosefoot" and it can be found in many locations. Pick the young leaves and the plant stems and boil them into a spinach-like meal. The seeds of this plant are very high in protein and if available in your area it makes a very good survival food.

These plants are just a few of the more common wild plants that can be eaten in a survival setting. The plants are easy to recognize and easy to prepare to eat. They can be found in a wide variety of habitats and climates.

It is important that you use caution whenever you are trying new plants to eat. It is always best to study these plants and try them before you are ever faced with a survival situation in which you are desperate to find food to eat.

You must be sure that you are identifying the correct plant to eat, and not something that looks similar but may be harmful to you.

Cooking Wild Birds And Other Game

All birds are edible. You can cook these after they are skinned and cleaned. One easy way to cook birds that have been skinned and cleaned is to just impale them on a green stick and hold the meat over a fire. You can set the stick over a stone to elevate the bird above the fire to cook. A second stone on the end of the stick will keep it secure. Roast the meat slowly over the fire as you attend to other chores.

Sear the meat on both sides to help lock in the meat juices then cook the meat over the fire rotating often until done. You can also cook the bird over a nice bed of hot coals that will allow you to not burn the meat with the open flame of the fire.

Another way to cook the bird is to use two "Y" sticks placed in the ground beside the fire. Place the bird on a green stick across the "Y" sticks, turning it occasionally to cook.

If you have a bird or other meat that you want to cook and rotate over the fire, you may want to tie a second stick to the end of the main green limb. When you attach the meat to both sticks, it will hold the meat much better and it will be easier to rotate over the fire.

When cooking any wild game the meat should only be cooked long enough to make it edible. The longer the meat is cooked the more nutrients are cooked out of the meat. If your survival diet is heavily meat, over cooking will eliminate much of the vitamin C that your body needs. Over cooking also tends to make the meat dry, and tough. It is best to sear the meat on all sides and then cook the meat until it is rare. The broth from boiled meat is very nutritious and good to drink.

Survival Cooking

When you are facing a survival situation and need to cook food, you first need to consider how to prepare the meal. Boiling a stew is probably the most popular method since it is very easy and you can continue to add to the stew pot with additional food items.

If you find yourself in a survival event and you do not have any cooking utensils you will need to improvise and make these to use. Fire can be used to make these essential cooking utensils.

You can make a cooking pot, a spoon or a cup from wood you find in the forest. Find a piece of wood that is solid and large enough to be crafted into the utensil you want. A large piece of wood that will hold a quart of liquid will make a very nice bowl for your survival needs.

The best woods to use are softwoods like cedar, pine, and firs. Hardwoods like oak and maple also work well but will take a bit more time to make. The hardwoods actually make a better container for liquids.

If you are able to find tree roots that are large enough for your utensil these work very well and do not have the problems of cracking like some woods do.

Use your hatchet to slice the piece of wood and get a flat surface. Chop the piece to an appropriate length. Carefully remove hot coals from your fire and set them in the center of your piece of wood. The hot coals will slowly burn into the wood. You will need to replace the coals several times to allow them to burn deep enough into the wood to make your container. Be sure to keep the coals in the center of the wood to keep them from burning out the edges. As the coals cool, blow on them to heat them up allowing them to burn further into the wood.

Depending on the type of wood you are using you should be able to burn out a piece of wood into a rough bowl in a few hours. You can repeat this process to make containers of various sizes.

When the container has been burned out you can then use your knife to finish cutting out the container to sculpture it into the shape you need.

To cook with these containers you can carefully remove a stone from the fire and place it into the container to quickly heat up your stew or water.

Seeds—Sprouting Your Own

We all know that seeds are vital to the reproduction of food that we eat. Many people however, are not aware of the incredible nutrition that sprouting seeds offer to your diet, and how easy it is to sprout your own seeds . . . all year long.

Seed sprouts are much more nutritious to eat than the dormant parent seed. Fresh sprouts are rich in protein, iron and have many vitamins.

Almost any seed can be sprouted and eaten, but there are a few important exceptions. You cannot sprout seeds from tomato, potato, paprika, aubergine, eggplant or rhubarb as the sprouts from these seeds are poisonous.

Sprouting whole grains and legumes are the most inexpensive type of seeds to use and they can be stored for long periods of time allowing you an excellent source of survival food. Only use fresh untreated whole seeds for sprouts. Certified organic seeds are best.

It is important that you do not use ordinary commercial seeds that are commonly used for planting in your garden for sprouting. These seeds are treated with a toxic fungicide chemical to protect the seed when it is initially planted. Even if the seeds are washed the sprouts can still have toxic levels of this fungicide.

When seeds sprout they increase in vitamins and protein and are an excellent supplement to any diet.

The process of sprouting seeds is quite simple and can be done at home in a makeshift environment. Seed sprouting will give you an excellent source of fresh vegetables all year.

Keeping a small supply of dry certified organic seeds for sprouting can be important in the event of a disaster. These seeds just need a very small amount of fresh water to grow. Consider keeping a variety of seeds in your emergency supply, and use the others to enjoy year around nutrition.

Sprouting seeds and eating raw sprouts does carry a risk. According to the U.S. Department of Health and Human Services eating raw sprouts can introduce food-borne bacteria into your food. Raw sprouts have been identified in many cases of food illness in the United States since 1996.

The reason for this is that most people enjoy eating sprouts raw rather than cooking them which kills any harmful bacteria. Growing sprouts thrive in a warm humid environment which is exactly the same environment in which bacteria is able to quickly grow and multiply.

Salmonella and E. coli are the two most common bacteria that are associated with eating raw sprouts whether they are grown commercially or at home. Salmonella has symptoms that include diarrhea, fever and abdominal cramps. Salmonella may become life threatening if the victim has a weakened immune system. E. coli is a disease that is generally developed from eating food that has been contaminated with cow feces. The symptoms are bloody diarrhea and abdominal cramps. E. coli can lead to compromised internal organs that can lead to death.

For those who want to eat fresh sprouts but not eat them raw, just cook the sprouts which will kill any harmful bacteria and makes them edible. Steam the sprouts or heat them to at least 165 degrees Fahrenheit to kill harmful bacteria.

Many growers believe that they can grow sprouts at home and are in better control of the growing environment than commercial sprout growers. To reduce the risk of growing any harmful bacteria be sure to only purchase certified pathogen-free sprouting seeds which have been tested for bacteria. Other seeds should not be used. Use only potable drinking water for your sprouts rather than non-potable irrigation water.

Home growers (as do commercial growers) can treat their seeds before sprouting by using a preheated solution of 3% hydrogen peroxide. Put the seeds in this solution and keep all of the seeds completely submerged for 5 minutes in temperatures of at least 140 degrees Fahrenheit. This helps kill any harmful bacteria that may be trapped in the crack of the seed and later develops into bacteria when the seed sprouts.

Always completely sanitize the sprouting containers and protect them from any outside contamination. Sanitation is the key to producing clean healthy sprouts.

What Seeds To Sprout?

Seeds such as alfalfa, oats, clover, oriental mustard, radish, mustard, dill, celery, red clover, sunflower, radish, leek and broccoli to name just a few.

Beans: Some of the favorite bean sprouts are Garbanzo, Lentil, Peanut, Adzuki and Pinto.

Grains: Wheat, buckwheat, barley, rye, millet and rice are a few.

Materials To Have

- * Clean glass jars with lid.

- * Cheese cloth and rubber band or a piece of fine screen that will fit inside the jar lid (cut to shape)

- * Quality seeds, legumes and grains—organic are best.

What To Do

After purchasing certified organic seeds, and properly chemically treating the seeds, follow these instructions:

1st Day: Put 2-3 tablespoons of seeds into the clean jar. Fill the jar with fresh water to cover the seeds several inches and allow them to soak overnight. The jar should be kept in a dark place at room temperature. When sprouting legumes double the soaking time as these are harder and require a longer soaking time.

2nd Day: The next morning rinse the seeds by pouring fresh water into the jar and then pouring it out through the cheese cloth or fine screen. Do this 2-3 times. Then drain all of the water out of the jar so that mold does not grow. Turn the jar on its top for a bit to insure that all of the water drains out.

Rinse the seeds 2-4 times a day. In warm weather you need to rinse the seeds more often. After each rinsing drain all the water out of the jar and return to a dark place at room temperature. After the second day you may begin to see some tiny sprouts beginning to form depending on the seed.

3rd Day: Your sprouts should be going great by now. Continue to rinse and drain in the morning, midday, and at night.

4th Day: If you see nice sprout tails on the seeds then you can move the jar into the light. Lay the jar on its side (more growing surface) in bright sunlight or on a window sill. You will be amazed how the sprouts grow in only a few hours. The more light the better.

Keep the sprouts in full light for the day. They should be lush green.

When harvested, store the sprouts in a sealed container in the refrigerator. The sprouts will keep for about one week or so but it is best to eat them as soon as possible for their tasty freshness. Cook if desired.

Continue your sprouting operation and you will have fresh vegetables every day with only a small amount of seeds. By timing your sprouting operation you can grow lush greens all year long.

Seeds can be sprouted in a number of ways. There are commercial sprouting bags that you use instead of glass jars. There are also sprouting trays that are used to sprout seeds. The good news is that seeds are very inexpensive and it takes very little time or equipment to grow an abundance of nutritious sprouts. Research seed sprouting and see if this is something that you are interested in doing to supplement your diet and to use in a survival situation.

Food Storage

Long ago people had to survive by storing much of their summer harvested food through the winter. If they were not successful in doing this they died.

Modern day cold storage, freezers and refrigerators dramatically enhanced the ability to easily and conveniently store food. Unfortunately, when a disaster happens and the electricity goes down we instantly lose this convenience.

In the event of a disaster your ability to properly store these provisions becomes extremely important.

As mentioned, if you stock a 2-3 week emergency supply of normal canned and packaged groceries you will be well furnished to deal with most short term disasters. But what if the disaster is larger? In a catastrophic disaster many experts predict that the power grid will be out for many months and in some areas for as long as a year. Repairs to freeways and major bridges will take many months to complete. Food and other supplies cannot be transported to these devastated areas over the highways or on damaged railroad lines.

Root Cellars

Root cellars have been around for many centuries to keep the summer harvest preserved for winter months. Having a place to store food when the power grid goes down is an important step to survival.

Root cellars are simple. They preserve food longer than if the food was left at normal ambient temperature. Root cellars dug into the ground have low temperatures. This will keep the food from freezing in the winter and from getting spoiled from the heat in the summer.

A wide variety of foods can be stored in a root cellar from jams and jelly, butter, cheese, and salted meats. Other foods will not last in a root cellar and will spoil in a short period of time.

The ideal temperature in a root cellar is between freezing (32 degrees) and 40 degrees Fahrenheit. Simply put, the cooler the food the longer it will last. Root cellars with a high humidity of 80-90% are ideal for keeping vegetables fresh and from drying out. This is accomplished with a wet floor. Root cellars with a concrete floor will have a much lower humidity, which is best for storage of dry goods. The best root cellars have two rooms to accommodate both types of food.

Many root cellars are simply dug into a hillside or are buried in the ground with stair access. Some people have used deep caves which have a constant cool temperature all year long and are not affected by the outside weather.

An adequate root cellar can be built in the basement of a house, along the outside foundation of a home or in the yard as a stand alone root cellar inside a small outbuilding. The goal is to dig a hole in the ground that will insulate the stored food from the outside temperature. The root cellar should be constructed to prevent rodents from gaining access to your stored food supply.

COLD WEATHER DANGERS

Frostbite

Frostbite is a serious injury to your body that is caused by freezing. A wind chill of -20 (F) degrees will cause frostbite in just 30 minutes. It generally affects a person's nose, ears, fingers and toes. The condition occurs when the skin has chilled to below the freezing point and ice crystals have formed in the tissue killing the cells. Frostbite can permanently damage the body and in severe cases lead to amputation of the frostbitten area.

You can detect frostbite by noticing a discoloration of the skin in cold temperatures. The skin will feel waxy and will be numb. In the early stages the skin will appear red. As the condition worsens the skin will turn white and will appear to be hard. Eventually the skin will blister and turn black.

In a survival situation where you cannot get immediate medical treatment get into a warm area as soon as possible.

If at all possible do not walk on feet that have been frostbitten as this will increase the damage to the skin and toes.

Gently expose the skin to warmth but not hot water. The skin will be numb and putting the skin too close to a fire or into hot water may further damage the skin since the victim will not feel any pain.

If you have frostbitten fingers, put them under your armpits to keep them warm.

The best way to avoid frostbite is to be properly prepared to deal with extreme cold temperatures. Wear proper clothing and avoid getting wet in extreme cold conditions.

Hypothermia

This is a condition that occurs when your body loses more heat than it produces resulting in your core body temperature dropping to dangerous levels. Hypothermia develops when the body temperature drops to less than 95 degrees Fahrenheit. Hypothermia is a deadly killer. Survivors are likely to have lifelong problems with their kidneys and liver.

Symptoms of hypothermia are:

* Mental confusion

* Slurred speech

* Uncontrolled shivering

* Loss of coordination

* Appearance of a puffy face

To treat hypothermia first get to a warm location where the body can warm up. Cover the person with blankets, clothing, bedding and anything else that will warm them up. Since most of the body heat is lost from the head, be sure to put on a heavy stocking cap, wool hat or wrap the head with clothing to keep warm.

Often hypothermia results from a person getting wet in very cold weather. If this happens be sure to get their wet clothing off as soon as possible and have them put on dry clothes. Hypothermia is a serious condition and can lead to death.

When medical attention is not available it is important to begin slowly warming the person starting with the core of the body. Rapidly warming the extremities (arms/legs) can force cold blood into the heart causing heart failure. Wrap the person in warm dry clothing. Be sure to cover the head and neck to retain body heat.

SHELTER

The other basic principal to survival is shelter.

In any survival situation you will eventually need to find a location where you can be sheltered from the weather and keep warm. You will need a place that allows you to be safe from injury, safe from wildlife, and safe from anyone or anything that may harm you.

If at home after a disaster any camping supplies including a tent will be a significant benefit for you and your family if your home is damaged and not inhabitable.

Assess the area you live in to decide what type of tent would be best to have in the event your home is destroyed or damaged to the extent that you cannot live there. Many inexpensive tents will do just fine in moderate weather. If you live in a windy area or in a cold climate you need to have a rugged tent that will meet these needs.

Your shelter needs to be an area where you can build fire to keep you warm, cook your food and boil your water. A fire not only offers you protection from the weather and wildlife but it also has the psychological boost of building your confidence particularly on a dark night. Building a shelter and tending a fire provides a sense of personal security, and has a calming effect in a time of dire circumstances.

Many of the shelter designs that are good for one climate are also good for another. When reviewing these various shelters think on how they could be used in other environments.

Where To Build Shelter

In cold weather conditions shelter becomes critical to your survival. It is important that you select a proper location to build the shelter. Look around to see what dangers may compromise your shelter. Building shelter in ravines or river beds that may suddenly be hit with a flash flood or on the side of a mountain clearing where avalanches are likely to happen is not the place to build your shelter. Try to make your shelter close to a water source if possible but well away from high tide.

If you are suddenly in a survival situation and you need an emergency shelter to protect you from rain, snow and the wind, focus all of your time and energy on that task before it gets too dark. It is much easier to make a shelter when you can see the area around you to collect available materials than it is stumbling around in the dark. If it is getting late, build a fire and then use the light from the fire to construct your shelter.

When building any shelter you should always try to build the best shelter you can with the least amount of time and energy. For this reason you need to use your ingenuity and the available resources around you.

As with any survival situation it is important that you carry with you those items necessary to make shelter. The items described for your bug-out-bag will work nicely for this purpose.

First, take a careful look around to see what natural objects are available that offer potential shelter. These objects can significantly reduce the time it takes to make a shelter.

One mistake many people make is to construct a large shelter. Do not make a large shelter. Make a shelter just large enough for you to get into. A small shelter will be much easier to heat, and it allows your body heat to help keep you warm.

A small fire is all you need in your shelter to keep warm during the night. Make your small fire near the opening and it will give sufficient heat all night. Be sure to bring in plenty of small dry firewood to tend to the fire during the night. It is always better to bring in more wood than you expect to use so you do not run out during the night.

Try to block much of the shelter's opening to reduce the heat from escaping and preventing the wind from blowing into your shelter. The opening should be sufficient to allow the smoke from the fire to escape. If possible make the entrance to your shelter away from prevailing winds.

When building any shelter be sure to collect enough dry materials to be used for bedding to insulate you from the ground. This bedding not only keeps you dry but it also allows you to get a comfortable night sleep instead of tossing and turning all night on the hard ground.

Types of Shelter

A fallen tree often leaves a large hole where the root ball was and the fallen tree offers a possible source of fire wood. Put down a good layer of browse or dry leaves in the hole. Lay branches over the hole and then throw leaves and boughs over the top at least 2-3 feet high. This makes a good roof that will afford some protection from rain and will hold the heat inside your shelter.

A group of fallen trees offers several locations where a small shelter can be made beside or under these trees. Find a good solid location and cover the floor area with dry materials.

Lay in additional branches for a roof to keep out the snow, rain and wind. Put additional green boughs on the sides to protect the shelter from the wind. This small shelter will keep you quite comfortable during the night with a small fire.

A deep cutout in a bank of soil makes a good overnight shelter during warm weather in an emergency. A large overhang ledge among large rocks will also work.

A sturdy branch lodged parallel between two trees makes the top for a simple "A" frame shelter. Stack boughs on all sides to make a shelter that protects you from the wind and rain. Cover the floor with a thick layer of fir boughs or dry leaves and you will be quite snug inside. If possible, construct the shelter with the opening facing away from the prevailing wind. Ideally the shelter will not be constructed with the back directly at the wind because the wind could blow and curl around the front of the shelter causing smoke from your fire to blow inside.

Always try to make the opening of the shelter a bit crosswise to any wind.

Take a stick and drag it around the outside of your shelter to make a shallow 2" ditch that will catch any rain water and run it away from your shelter. This only takes a few minutes to do but you will be glad you took the time to keep the inside of your shelter dry.

Snow Caves And Snow Shelter

In an emergency you can make shelter in the snow that will protect you from the elements. Take a look around to see what is available to make a snow shelter. You may find a naturally protected area under a fallen tree or an area of trees that have been blown down making hollow areas that are large enough for you to get into for shelter.

Look for large trees that have low-hanging snow covered limbs. Often these trees have a nice space under these limbs that can be made into a shelter. Once inside you can shape the snow and create an area that will give you insulation from the cold. Place tree boughs or other forest materials on the floor to insulate you from the ground. If you build a fire keep it small. You will only need a small fire in this confined area to keep warm. Be careful that the heat from the fire does not melt heavy snow from the branches above that may fall on you.

Sometimes you may need to dig into these snow pockets to find shelter. Put dry material down on the ground and be sure that you have adequate ventilation in the top. Make a fist size hole or two with a stick through the snow roof to keep a good exchange of oxygen in your shelter.

If you locate a rocky snow covered area you can dig a snow shelter between two large boulders. Dig into the snow and block the opening with boughs and your pack.

If you find a large snow drift or snow bank, dig into the snow and make an area large enough for you to get into and sit upright comfortably. Cover the floor with tree boughs or other material that will insulate you from the ground. Use a stick to poke a couple of fist size holes through the roof area so you can get fresh air. Place additional fir boughs to cover the entrance to help keep the wind out. Take your backpack and block the entrance.

When digging snow shelters in a snow bank or snow drift, try to begin at a low point in the drift and dig slightly upward to the area where you will stay. This slightly elevated area will help trap body heat in the shelter and also help protect the interior from the wind.

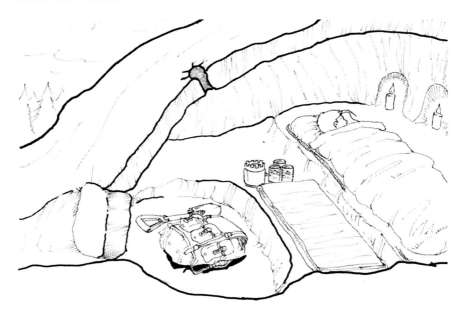

Snow caves are good protection from the weather. Put as much material down on the floor as you need to protect you from the cold and from getting wet.

You are likely to find snow that may be soft and dry or heavy and wet. Regardless of the type of snow that you encounter, you will be able to make a good snow shelter to keep you out of the elements. A very small fire will warm your shelter nicely.

If you do not have a shovel to dig your snow shelter, find a piece of wood that will work as a rough shovel. If necessary use your metal cooking pot to dig out your shelter. If at all possible do not use your hands to dig a snow shelter as the cold snow will quickly freeze your hands causing serious health problems.

Snow Trench

You can make a snow trench for shelter in much the same manner as you make a trench shelter for the desert.

When you are in an area with no trees and heavy snow, dig a trench about 3 feet deep and a bit longer than your body. Dig the trench crosswise to the wind. As you dig the trench place the displaced snow on the side of the trench that will block the wind. Tamp this snow down to make a good wind barrier. Put dry material in the bottom of the trench. If you have the plastic sheet, this makes a good barrier to keep you from getting wet. Even a plastic garbage bag will work for this purpose.

Roof the trench with your tarp, sheets of plastic, or garbage bags from your bug-out-bag. Anchor down all edges with packed snow. Put a layer of snow on the roof as thick as you can without causing the roof to collapse. The snow over the roof will provide good insulation for the shelter. Leave a small opening at one end for you to crawl into. Use some snow from inside the trench to partially block this entrance to help trap your body heat inside the shelter.

Carbon Monoxide Poisoning

It is important to remember that heating and cooking in snow shelters, tents and other confined areas have caused many deaths from carbon monoxide poisoning. Carbon monoxide is both odorless and cumulative. The effects of carbon monoxide slowly build up during normal breathing until the person is overcome by this poison and dies.

Do not use wood fires, stoves or gas lanterns inside snow caves or other closed shelters. When you need to cook put your stove just outside the snow shelter to cook and boil water. It is always good to have a couple of fist sized open air holes in the roof of your snow shelter at all times that will provide a good exchange of fresh air. You should be able to burn a candle in your snow shelter with this ventilation. Check these air holes frequently to make sure snow fall does not plug them up.

Tarp Shelter

If you have your **tarp** use it to fabricate a nice waterproof shelter using either the "A" frame method, or by hanging the tarp over a rope or line that has been stretched between two trees. Secure the tarp to the ground at the corners with small wooden pegs. Cover the floor with dry leaves, fir boughs, plastic sheeting or other material and you will have a very comfortable shelter. For additional insulation, pile large quantities of dry leaves and boughs around and over the top of the tarp. Use the tarp flap at one end and you have a convenient door that you can close to hold the heat in and keep cold air out.

Use the **10' x 10' sheet of painter's plastic** to make shelter. This will make a good shelter to protect you from the wind and rain. Place the sheet of plastic over a depression in the ground and then pile a thick layer of leaves or boughs on the top and crawl inside. The plastic will keep rain and snow from leaking into your shelter. It also is a good barrier to keep the wind from blowing through your shelter. Add dry material to the ground for insulation.

If you are short on time you can simply make a large 6' pile of dead leaves and then wrap the plastic around you and bury yourself under the pile of leaves. The plastic will trap your body heat and keep you from getting wet. The leaves you lay on in this pile will insulate you from the ground.

You can make a warm shelter in cold weather using the tarp or the sheet of plastic. Find a suitable depression in the ground large enough for you to lie in. Build a fire in the depression and cook your food and disinfect your water. When ready to sleep, remove the coals from the depression and lay down a bed of green browse. Cover the top of the depression as previously described and you will have a very warm shelter even in extreme cold weather. The walls of the depression will keep the bedding from moving around and you should be quite comfortable. You may want to bring in a few medium size stones that were in the fire to add additional heat in your shelter during the night.

An **emergency space blanket** makes an excellent shelter. It is small and easy to carry. The "space blanket" will also reflect heat from a fire to keep you warm.

Moisture is a killer in extreme cold temperatures. In cold temperatures prepare any shelter to keep you from getting wet. This is critically important to your survival.

You will find that getting a good night sleep will make your life much easier. It is a mistake to not get good sleep in a survival situation. For that you need good shelter. If you do not get enough sleep you will soon become exhausted and begin making poor decisions that may compromise your survival efforts.

Jungle Shelter

For surviving in a jungle environment you need to carry items that will help you survive for that specific climate.

The same basic principles of shelter apply in the jungle with one exception. It is probably better to get well off the ground in that environment to avoid things that crawl and things that go bump in the night. Hanging your tarp like a hammock in a tree may not be the most comfortable shelter that you have ever had but it probably is the safest for jungle survival.

If you do not have a tarp, or other material suitable for sleeping on then improvise and make a woodwork with branches and vines that will support your weight. Place that into a tree between branches for sleeping.

You can also find those natural areas where you can improvise a shelter for the night. In some areas you can find large rock formations that will offer areas where you can improve and make a suitable shelter. Caves may be also available in these areas.

You can make shelter from bamboo by using the same techniques as discussed earlier.

Heavy jungle grass and vegetation can be used to make a comfortable bed in a secure area.

Make the best shelter that you can. If you made a temporary shelter continue to use that as you then build a much better shelter for extended use.

Alan Corson

Desert Shelter

In the desert you are facing a much different set of survival circumstances. In these situations you want to avoid as much sun as possible. On other occasions you may be facing bitter freezing cold or snow.

Desert shelter can be very similar to the techniques that are used in other environments. Change the design to fit the circumstances.

Visually search your surroundings. Look for natural objects that will give you some type of shade even for part of a day.

In hot weather in an open desert, make a desert shelter by digging a trench into the ground. Make the trench somewhat wider than your chest and about three feet deep. Position the trench running in a north/south direction to keep as much sunlight off of you as possible.

Positioning yourself into the bottom of the trench can reduce the temperature there as much as 90-100 degrees from surface ground area. This reduced temperature can save your life. If possible throw a piece of clothing or other material over the trench to further shade you from the sun. To further increase the shade try to place a second object such as a layer of clothing a foot or so above the clothing covering the trench. This will deflect more heat from the clothing covering your trench, which will keep you cooler.

In many desert situations if you can bury yourself into the sand you can protect yourself from a scorching sun and sunburn. This will reduce your dehydration as well.

If you are able to find any desert object such as a tree or rock formation or group of cactus, you can use these objects to shield you from the sun and use their shade.

An emergency space blanket can be used to improvise a cover over a small depression in the ground. The sunlight will deflect from the silver material on the blanket, and keep the area in the depression cool.

To make shade, tie the emergency blanket to an object several feet off the ground such as a boulder or cactus, and spread out the end of the blanket to create a nice area of shade.

The desert at night can change dramatically and what was an extremely hot day may become a very chilled night.

If you are traveling on foot in the desert you probably will want to travel at night and lay up during the heat of the day.

In any desert situation always look for ravines and large rock outcroppings that may offer the means of making shelter. A cave is an excellent desert shelter. If you are fortunate to locate a large deep cave you will find that interior temperature to be quite cool and refreshing. These caves also frequently have water sources nearby.

When using any cave for shelter be sure that you make a diligent search for any wildlife that may be using the cave that could harm you. Look closely for snakes, scorpions, or other wildlife in the cave. Look for tracks in the sand to see if animals are using the cave.

Also be careful about venturing too far into caves. Large caves often have numerous chambers where you could easily get lost and unable to find your way out.

Bats frequent caves and bat guano (droppings) in large quantities can be toxic for you to breathe.

The air quality deep inside caves can also be poor and cause you to become nauseated and sick. You could die deep inside a cave from a lack of oxygen. If you are using a candle for light and you see the flame begin to dim significantly on its own, the air may lack oxygen or have an excess of carbon dioxide. Leave that area immediately.

NAVIGATION

When faced with a survival situation you will need to make critical decisions for your survival. Depending on your circumstances you must decide whether it is best to remain where you are or leave to reach safety. Part of your decision will depend on your ability to navigate effectively whether you use natural features around you or with a map and compass. You need to be able to effectively navigate through various terrains to move safely from one location to another.

Anyone traveling into the wilderness should have a map and a good compass. With that basic equipment you will be able to navigate successfully in the direction that you want to travel. The more proficient you are with the map and compass the more precise your navigation and travel will be.

Determining Direction

If you are in a situation where you do not have a compass, you can still get a very good understanding of direction.

There are many methods that can be used to determine direction. You can use the sun, moon, stars, wind and even plants to help you determine direction. These methods will give you a general idea of direction and will help you to navigate without a compass and map.

Basic navigation begins with the fact that the sun rises generally in the east and sets generally in the west. The sun does not rise or set precisely in either of these directions except for a couple of times a year. There is also a seasonal variation to this pattern.

Sun Shadow Method

To find directions with this method find a straight stick about 3' long. The stick should be thick enough to cast a good shadow.

Find a level piece of ground in a sunny area. Place the stick into the ground so that it is standing straight up. Mark the tip of the shadow on the ground with a small stone or twig. This first shadow always marks WEST . . . everywhere on earth.

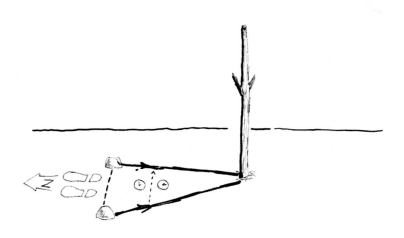

Wait for about 20 minutes or so. The shadow will move a few inches from the first mark. Put a stone or twig at the tip of the second shadow.

Draw a straight line between the two marks and you will have the approximate East/West direction.

Now stand with the heels of your feet in front of both shadow marks, having the sun at your back. You are now facing North. This is true for everywhere on earth.

Use a Watch For Direction

An analog watch can be used to determine general direction. The watch needs to have accurate time for the local area where you are located.

Put the watch on a level surface. The ground or a tree stump will do. Point the hour hand of the watch toward the sun. To be accurate you may need to get down and sight past the hour hand toward the sun. Then divide the angle between the hour hand and the 12 o'clock position. This will give you the North/South line. You can be sure which direction is north and which is south if you just remember that the sun rises in the east and sets in the west. Look where the sun is and you will easily determine which direction is north and which direction is south.

To quickly check direction while on the move you can simply point the hour hand of the watch at the sun and divide the angle between the 12 o'clock position to find your North/South line.

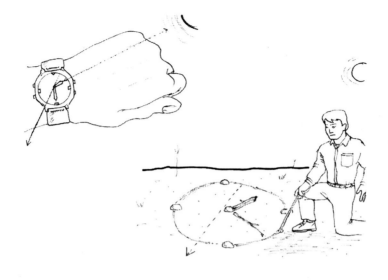

What if I have a digital watch?

If you have a digital watch you still can use this method. Use a pencil and paper, a smooth area on the ground or draw a watch in the snow. Put the correct time in the drawing with the hour hand pointing to the sun's position, and use it in the same manner to determine your direction. This technique is surprisingly accurate.

Southern Hemisphere—Watch Method

If you are in the southern hemisphere point the 12 o'clock position of the watch toward the sun. Use the midway point between the 12 o'clock position and the hour hand of the watch to find the North/South line.

Navigating at Night

Northern Hemisphere—Constellations

At night you can use the stars to help navigate and determine your location. The primary constellations that you need to learn and be able to find in the night sky are the Big Dipper and Cassiopeia. These two constellations never set and they are always visible in a clear night sky.

Use these two constellations to locate Polaris or the North Star. The best way to locate the North Star is to locate the Big Dipper which usually can be seen on a clear night. The two stars on the outer edge of the Big Dipper point to Polaris. There are no bright stars between these pointing stars and the North Star.

If you can find Cassiopeia or the big "W" in the sky, the North Star is always the same angle from Cassiopeia. Cassiopeia has five stars that form the shape of a "W." The "W" may appear to be on its side. Locate the North Star straight out from the center of Cassiopeia.

The North Star forms part of the Little Dipper's handle. It is best to use both the Big Dipper and Cassiopeia to be sure that you have found the North Star. The Big Dipper and Cassiopeia are always found directly opposite of each other in the night sky. They rotate counterclockwise around Polaris with Polaris being in the center.

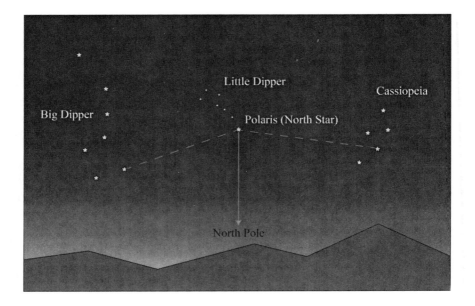

When viewing a night sky, if you see the stars moving from your right to left you are looking north. If you see the stars rising on the horizon then you are facing east. If you see stars moving from your left to right you are facing south. If you see stars falling on the horizon you are facing west.

At night you can carefully line up two sticks in the ground with both tips pointing to Polaris (North Star). This will give you a north pointing direction the following morning.

Southern Hemisphere—Constellation

In the southern sky there is no bright star that is easy to recognize near the south celestial pole. The best way to find south without a compass is to find the constellation known as the Southern Cross. This constellation has five stars. The four brightest stars form a tilted cross in the sky. There are two stars that make up the cross's long axis and these can be used as pointer stars.

To determine the direction of South, visualize a line about five times the distance between these stars and that point is the general direction of south. At night you can place two sticks into the ground to line up this direction and the following morning you will have a line indicating the general direction of south.

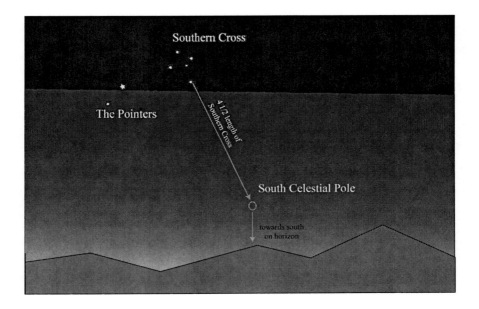

Compass

A compass is simply a device that has an enclosed magnetized needle that is free to float in a fluid. Due to the magnetism of the earth the needle will naturally orientate itself to magnetic North direction.

Parts

The compass housing has a rotating bezel on its base that is marked with numbered "bearings" or "degrees." These numbers make up a 360 degree circle on the compass (North = 0, East = 90, South = 180, West = 270).

A compass will have a "direction of travel" arrow etched on the base plate which indicates the direction that you should walk when using the compass. Inside the compass you will find a red orientating arrow that is etched into the base of the compass. This red arrow aligns with "N" or north on the compass housing.

"Boxing The Compass" is a term that simply means turning the compass bezel until the red floating magnetic needle aligns over the larger red orientating arrow that is permanently fixed in the base of the compass. For example, when you are facing North and the "N" is at the top of the compass, the red magnetic arrow is aligned over the red orientating arrow in the compass.

Types Of Compasses

There are several types of compasses. There are very small button type compasses that are about the size of a nickel. These are very inexpensive compasses that do not have moving bezels or other advanced navigation parts. These compasses just have direction arrows and some smaller degree markings. Larger orienteering compasses have more advanced features such as a base plate and rotating bezel to make navigating easier and more accurate. Lensatic compasses are excellent for navigation.

These compasses have a rotating bezel, base and a lid that opens to allow for sighting to a distant point offering more precise navigation. The more advanced compasses also have the ability to adjust for area declination.

A good compass is a vital piece of equipment that may save your life if you know how to use it effectively. It is best to have a compass with a luminous dial for night navigation.

Many individuals like to carry a primary lensatic compass and a small backup compass such as the orienteering compass or even a button compass.

In winter navigation keep your compass warm inside your clothing. You can expect the needle to move sluggishly from the cold so allow more time to take a bearing.

One important rule to always follow when using a compass is to make sure that the compass is not used close to any metal such as in or on a motor vehicle. Do not use a compass around electronic equipment like radios or power lines as this may result in the compass giving an inaccurate reading. Occasionally you may walk over an area rich in iron ore and that too will affect the ability of your compass to operate correctly.

To operate a compass, always hold it level to allow the needle to freely float and settle on a marked bearing. Hold the compass at eye level to get a more accurate reading.

When the compass needle stops it will be pointing to "magnetic north." To orient yourself hold the compass steady and turn your whole body (not just the compass) with the compass held at eye level until you are lined up with the compass needle facing magnetic north. When you know the direction of north you know that east is to your right, south is directly behind you and west is to your left. Look for objects in the distance in each of these directions to help you orientate yourself to your environment.

Magnetic Declination & Maps

A compass is influenced by the earth's magnetic field which makes the compass needle line up with "magnetic north." Maps however, are orientated to the "true north" or the North Pole. There is a difference between these two points and that difference is referred to as "declination." This variance must be calculated when using a compass with a map to navigate.

When holding the compass level the magnetic needle will freely float and come to rest pointing to "magnetic north." The problem is that "true north" (North Pole) is different from "magnetic north" which is what your compass will read. For this reason you need to adjust your compass for the "declination" in the specific area that you are located. Declination varies depending on your location in the world. This adjustment is simply the difference between what your compass needle is reading (magnetic north) and true north.

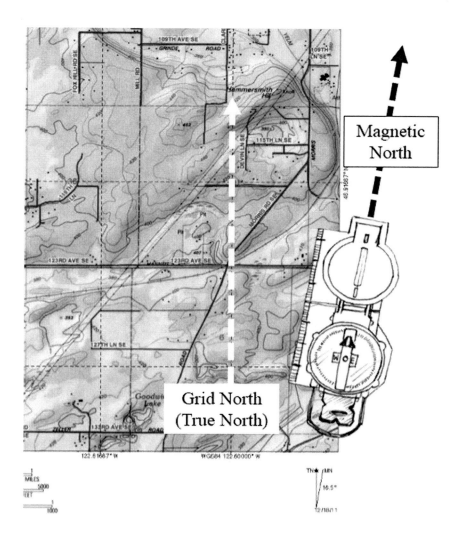

Topographical Maps

Topographical maps are detailed maps that give information about the land features in a given area. These maps include manmade structures, and natural features such as mountains, rivers and roads.

There are many different types of maps but the best maps to use when navigating are topographical maps. When using a topographical map it is important to understand the legend and map scale. Maps list the scale in the legend on the map. Some maps have a scale of 1:250,000 which means that one unit on this map (inches, feet, meters, kilometers) equals 250,000 units. Most USGA maps use a 1:24,000 scale where one inch equals 2,000 feet or 2.64 inches represents one mile. Understanding the scale on a map will greatly aid you in navigating from one point to another.

Topographical maps have "contour lines." These are the most distinguishing features on the map. These are lines on a map connecting points of equal elevation. These lines are used to show elevation and the general shape of the terrain at specific locations on the map.

When the contour lines are very close together the elevation is very steep. When the contour lines are far apart the elevation in that area is relatively flat. The gradual widening of these lines indicates the slop of the terrain. Correctly reading topographical maps and contour lines will let you understand the terrain you are facing when you navigate from one point to another. This allows you to choose the best route for you to reach your destination. Taking the path of least resistance, and avoiding those hazardous areas that are located on the map, will significantly enhance your travels.

When navigating with the use of a map always study the scale on the map to understand the distances and terrain where you are navigating. Carefully study the map's information and distance to determine if you can navigate to the intended landmarks in the amount of time that you have. If you calculate incorrectly you may find yourself unable to reach your destination and you will spend the night in the wild.

Most topographical maps will provide the declination for that area. When using the map adjust the compass for declination in that area. You can also find magnetic declination for specific areas on charts where maps are sold or on the Internet.

You can successfully use a compass that does not have built in declination. Learn the degree of declination in the area you are navigating, and then make that degree of adjustment on your compass when taking a reading. You add or subtract that number of degrees when making your navigational calculations from your map.

If you have a compass that can be manually set to compensate for the declination just make that adjustment on the compass according to the area you are in. From that point on just read the bearing on the compass to navigate. Since the earth's magnetic fields are constantly changing over time, find and use the most current declination information when navigating.

The first step when using a compass and map is to orientate your map with your compass and your location.

To do this, dial your compass so the "N" (north) is at the top. Lay the map on a flat (non-metallic) surface. Place your compass on the map with the needle facing north. Turn the map under the compass until the north/south grid lines match up with the compass needle and north is indicated on the compass. The map is now orientated to magnetic north.

Then turn the map slowly until the needle on the compass indicates the amount of magnetic declination that is given for that area. Again, this declination is generally indicated on the map in the legend.

For example, if the map legend indicates "12 degrees east" of declination, then true north is not where the needle on the compass indicates but instead 12 degrees east of that needle mark.

You have now orientated the map to the real world and if you know your location on the map it should be easy for you to see various objects and landmarks depicted on the map in the correct direction from your location.

You can use your compass at night to check the compass declination. Point the compass needle at the North Star and check the luminous dial to see how close the needle is from the North Star. The difference between the North Star and where the needle of your compass indicates will be the local magnetic declination.

You can then set your compass with this declination to more accurately use the map.

Using A Compass To Navigate

There are several ways to use a compass to navigate from one point to another. Each of these techniques will require you to "box the compass" which, again means holding the compass steady and turning the compass bezel until it aligns over the red orientating arrow in the compass. Be sure to always point the compass in the direction in which you want to travel (use the pointing arrow on compass base).

In the wilderness for example, if you see a distant location that you want to travel to, here is what you need to do:

1. First use your compass to locate north. All bearings on the compass originate from the position of north so it is always good to start from that position. Box the compass to the direction of north.

2. Next, hold the compass level, and up at eye level. Turn your whole body (holding the compass in front of your face) and point the compass to the distant point where you want to go. If the compass has a "V" sight, use that to visually pinpoint the distant object.

While you are sighting with the compass at the distant point, slowly rotate the compass bezel and "box the compass." Continue rotating the bezel until you line up the magnetic red needle with the red orientation arrow in the compass. This gives you the bearing or "magnetic azimuth" that you need to follow to reach your destination.

It is always a good idea to check this process several times with the compass to insure that you have gotten the same correct bearing before starting off on your journey.

Now that you have the compass bearing that you will follow, look along that bearing and find a closer landmark between you and your final destination (you may find several of these depending on how far you need to go). Use the compass bearing to walk to those landmarks on the line to your final destination. At times you may lose sight of this landmark. Use the compass with the established bearing and walk forward keeping the magnetic arrow over the underlying red alignment arrow. It is easier to pick out a closer landmark on that same bearing and walk to it and then continue the journey with another landmark along the compass bearing until you reach your destination.

If you are using your compass to simply take and follow bearings from one point to another you can disregard map declination. If you are just using a map to navigate and use compass bearings from one point to another, declination will not be important. Declination does become important if you calculate map bearings from a map which is drawn to true north and then use those map bearings to navigate with your compass. Several degrees difference from declination will throw you a substantial distance off and you may miss reaching your intended destination.

After you reach your destination how do you get back to where you started?

Back Azimuth

To return to your original location you simply follow the opposite direction that is set on the compass. For example, if the compass was set for north (360 or zero degrees) the opposite bearing on the compass would be 180 degrees or south. A 90 degree compass bearing would have a 270 degree compass back azimuth. Back azimuth simply means the opposite direction of the direction set on your compass. Simply add or subtract 180 on your compass setting to get your back azimuth. Then dial that new bearing on your compass, sight along that bearing and repeat the navigation process.

Finding Your Location On The Map

Triangulation

You can use your compass to locate your position on a topographical map. This will give you the ability to know where you are on the map, locate landmarks that you can see, and then be able to navigate from that location.

Study the map to see where your location may be such as along a river, ridge line or road. You will be able to find your position with just that information as long as you can see another landmark that is depicted on the map such as a mountain peak, rock outcropping, structure or other mapped landmark.

Take a careful compass bearing from your location to the landmark and read that bearing on your compass. Since you are transferring a compass bearing to a map grid, you want to SUBTRACT the magnetic declination (listed on the map) from this bearing, leaving you with the corrected bearing to transfer to the map.

Dial in this corrected bearing on the compass. Place the top left edge of the compass base plate over the landmark on the map. Keeping the edge of the compass on the landmark, rotate the whole compass base (not the compass bezel dial) until the compass meridian lines are aligned with the vertical grid lines on the map. Then draw a line from the landmark along the base of the compass to intersect with the river, road or location where you are walking. The intersection of these points will be your location.

If you are in a place that does not have a landmark for your location, you can still find your location on the map. You do this by locating two distant landmarks that you can see and recognize on the map. The farther these two landmarks are apart, the more accurate your reading will be.

Take a bearing on the first landmark. Make necessary declination adjustments to the compass bearing and set that bearing on the compass. Orientate the compass in the same manner as above with the first landmark. Draw a line along the base plate of the compass. Then take a bearing on the second landmark using the same corrected declination. Draw a line along the base of the compass from the second landmark. The intersection of these two lines will be your location on the map.

You can use a third or fourth landmark in the same way to obtain an even more accurate verification of your location.

This process works best if you find two landmarks that are about 90 degrees apart.

You can use triangulation to be able to return to an exact location such as your camp. Find two good landmarks and take compass bearings on each. Record these two (or more) bearings. When returning to the area simply position yourself where these two bearings intersect and you will find your camp.

Being able to navigate with a map and compass will be extremely important particularly if you are navigating and adverse weather sets in blocking visibility. In those instances your ability to read a compass and map can save your life.

Making Your Own Compass

While this may have marginal benefit for a person navigating a long distance, it does have the benefit of giving you a general direction when you do not have a compass so that you do not walk for days and end up walking in a circle, returning to the place where you started.

To make a compass you will need a small sewing needle, piece of paperclip, or other sliver of ferrous metal. Stroke the needle continuously in a single direction in your hair for a minute or so. This will magnetize the needle. You can also use a scrap piece of silk or you can magnetize the needle in the same manner if you have a small magnet.

Next, locate a tiny pool of water. Take a small green leaf or a couple of blades of grass and place the needle on them. Carefully put this into the pool of water causing them to float. Allow the floating needle to slowly rotate until it stops. The direction of the needle will be the north/south direction. If you stroked the needle carefully from the eye of the needle to the tip the eye of the needle will point to north.

WEATHER DISASTERS

Floods

Floods are one of the most prolific killers in the world. Flooding can occur almost anywhere and in the United States it is the most common disaster that we encounter.

How to Prepare

There are a few important ways to prepare for a flood. If you live in an area that is known to be susceptible to floods you may want to have a boat or emergency life raft handy at your home. Also keep life jackets handy for all members of your family. Flash floods happen quickly and you may only have time to get to a life jacket or life raft before the flood waters rise to dangerous levels.

Sandbags To Avoid Flood Water

Sandbags can be used in low-lying areas to redirect flood water away from your home when you have advanced warning. This project works best with two people. You can use burlap sandbags or plastic sandbags made from polypropylene. Both work well.

1. Gather all of the supplies you will need. Sandbags, shovel, sheet of heavy polyurethane plastic or tarps will do. Also get a wheelbarrow to transport the filled sandbags.

2. Fill the sandbags about half full with sand. They should weigh about 40 pounds each when filled.

3. If possible dig a shallow trench in line where you want to stop the water. This trench should be 6" deep and 18"-24" wide.

4. Place the heavy plastic sheeting or tarp in the trench and secure with sandbags.

5. Begin a row of sandbags in the trench with the ends of the bags overlapping. Stagger the next row to cover the spaces in the first row. Continue to build the stack until the right height. Then begin another row of sandbags behind this first pile. Overlap the sandbags as you build the wall. When that is finished begin another row in front of the first row, building a thick wall that will keep the majority of the flood water out. Limit your stack to about three layers of sandbags because any more will make the pile unstable.

This is a simple but effective way to prevent or reduce water damage. This will not provide a watertight seal but will divert water from your home or property.

If you are under a flood watch or warning

Gather your emergency supplies that you have previously stocked in your home and put them in an area where they are immediately accessible. These need to be instantly available if you suddenly need to leave home.

These supplies include:

* At least 5-10 gallons of water. More if you have several members of the family

* 7-10 day supply of non-perishable food and a hand can opener

* Your home first-aid kit and all prescriptions and medicine

* Camping gear including tent, cooking stove, fuel, pots & pans, and utensils

* Flashlights and extra supply of batteries (better yet, hand crank—no battery flashlights)

* Sleeping bags, blankets and other bedding as necessary

* Iodine, chlorine bleach, or commercial water purification device

* Hand crank (battery free) radio with NOAA capability

* Matches, lighter, fire steel and/or magnesium fire starter and tinder

* Knife and hatchet

* Personal hygiene for each member of the family

* Extra clothes for each member of the family

* Proper shoes and boots

* Car emergency kit

* Other items as may be necessary for you and your family

** See items listed in Priority One, Two and Three

Keep a careful watch on the weather during storm conditions. Make sure you are able to receive weather reports even if your power is out. A **battery-free crank radio** with NOAA will provide you with constant weather conditions for your location.

With any flood warning you need to anticipate the need to evacuate. Plan and prepare for it.

* Keep your vehicle's fuel tank full.

* Make sure you have your vehicle emergency kit in your vehicle.

* Put important papers and documents in a waterproof container to bring with you.

* Discuss your emergency evacuation plans, where you are going and these details with all family members.

* Make telephone calls to let family and friends know of you plans.

* Leave a detailed note in your home to notify rescue personnel when you left, where you are going, and when you expect to arrive. Include emergency telephone numbers.

* Be ready to leave immediately if you are directed to do so by authorities.

* Monitor the route that you plan to take to be sure it is open and not closed due to flooding. Have several alternate routes to use if necessary.

If authorities give warnings to leave an area threatened by a flood, comply with those directives and leave. There is nothing in your home worth dying for.

If you need to evacuate and have time, turn off the electricity at the main utility box in your home. Turn off the gas valve if your home has one.

When driving in areas with heavy rainfall or in flood conditions use extra caution to insure that your vehicle is not swept off the road. It only takes a few inches of water to cause your vehicle to hydroplane and not much more rushing water to sweep your vehicle off the road. Floods cause many deaths each year when people try to drive their vehicles through deep flood water. Flash floods are a major reason for deaths. The majority of these deaths occur when people walk or drive a vehicle into flood waters.

Hurricanes

Every year hurricanes cause an enormous amount of damage and death around the world. Hurricanes should not be taken lightly with the belief that it is just a wind storm. Tropical storms have proven to be killers and can and do wreak havoc across a wide area.

Hurricanes cause downed power grids, flash floods, and severe damage to homes and businesses.

If you are directed to evacuate because of a pending hurricane, comply and get out as soon as possible. Do not wait until the last minute to try to escape or you may be unable to do so.

If you are able to safely stay in your home (and have not been directed to leave) you must be prepared to survive at least 10-15 days without having access to outside food, water or electricity. That means you need all of the necessary things to survive without any outside help for a minimum of 10-15 days. Check your emergency supply carefully to see if you have sufficient rations. In catastrophic hurricanes you can expect to be without electricity, utilities, and food services for several months or longer. Plan accordingly.

In many instances you will have a warning of a pending storm or other severe weather event. If you are able to safely remain in your home by all means prepare to hunker down for the storm.

You should stay inside your home on the first floor. Keep away from all windows and glass doors as these may shatter with considerable force during the storm. Try to stay in a small interior room that does not have windows. Lie on the floor under or near a sturdy object such as a heavy table, desk or couch. These offer some protection from heavy falling objects.

Be sure you have flashlights or battery lanterns available in the storm. Do not use anything with an open flame such as a candle or hurricane lamp during the storm. Many homes have been destroyed during storms from open flames.

It is always a good idea to add to your stored water supply before the storm hits by filling your bathtub, sink, large pots and other convenient containers with tap water. You can use this fresh water first in any emergency and then if necessary resort to your stored water reserves. Always plan on collecting additional water as soon as possible after any disaster.

To prepare for this storm you will need the same items that you normally need for camping out where you do not have fresh tap water, restaurants for food or electricity for several days or weeks. Plan on camping out at home for an extended period of time.

The home emergency items previously listed should be on hand for any disaster.

Being prepared in your home:

1. If you have hurricane shutters have the parts ready to securely close them. If you need to board up the windows with plywood have the supplies ready and don't wait until the last minute or you may not be able to finish the task.

2. Remove anything from your yard that can blow in the wind and cause damage.

3. Make sure everyone in the family is aware of your home disaster plan and where the first aid supplies are kept.

4. Make sure you know how to turn off the valve for the natural gas, or propane in your home. Also be familiar with the main electrical box in the home to shut off the electricity if necessary. Keep necessary tools available in case of an emergency. This is a very important step in preventing home fires. If you need to turn off your natural gas do NOT turn it back on.

5. Be sure you are familiar with the main water valve for your home and have the tools to shut off the water if necessary to prevent flooding. Shutting off this water valve will help keep pollutants out of your water line and allow you to have some drinking water in the lines.

6. In any wind storm (hurricane or tornado) it is important to protect your body as much as possible. Many injuries occur from head trauma. If possible put on a bicycle helmet, motorcycle helmet, hard hat or similar head gear to protect from falling debris and glass. Put on heavy leather gloves to protect your hands from broken glass and other sharp objects.

Put on a heavy leather coat to protect your upper body from flying debris and sharp objects. A good pair of leather boots will help protect your feet and ankles from broken glass and sharp objects.

Tornadoes

Tornadoes are one of nature's most violent storms. They originate from thunderstorms and frequently cause death and devastation in a matter of minutes.

A tornado appears as a rotating funnel cloud that extends from a thunderstorm down to the ground. Winds can reach nearly 300 miles per hour. The damage from a tornado can exceed a mile wide and as much as 50 miles long. Not all tornadoes are visible. Rain or low clouds may hide the tornado until it strikes. These violent storms usually occur near the trailing edge of a powerful thunderstorm.

Tornadoes will occasionally accompany tropical storms and hurricanes.

What To Do During A Tornado

At Home:

* If you are at home and receive a tornado warning immediately go to a safe room or approved tornado shelter area. These shelters should be part of your home disaster plan so everyone knows what to do and where to go if this emergency happens.

* If you do not have a designated tornado shelter, go to an area in your home that has no windows such as in a basement, bathroom or closet. You are better off in the lowest level of the home as winds will have more effect on second and third stories.

* Get under a heavy piece of furniture such as a desk.

* If you have bedding available take that to help shield you from debris during the storm. A heavy bed mattress would make a good shield.

* Sit down and hold your hands to protect your head and neck. Take the same precautions for wearing head gear, coat, gloves and boots to protect you from falling debris.

* If you live in a mobile home immediately get out and find proper shelter somewhere else. You will not be safe in a mobile home during a tornado!

At Work:

* Most employers have a designated area to have employees go in the event of a tornado. Go there as soon as possible.

* If you cannot get to a designated tornado shelter at work try to find appropriate shelter nearby that is tornado approved. If not, get into a building on ground level and away from any glass. Get under a large heavy piece of equipment or furniture.

* Use heavy furniture to protect you from flying debris.

If Outdoors

If you find yourself outside when a tornado is approaching immediately seek appropriate shelter inside a suitable building.

If you cannot reach a building find a ditch or deep depression in the ground and lay there. A culvert may provide good temporary shelter but watch out for flooding.

If you are in a car

* Never try to drive closer to see a tornado as it approaches. Incredible as this advice may sound, some people actually drive toward tornados so they can get a better look and maybe take pictures. These storms are unpredictable and can change directions quickly. If they do, you may not be able to outrun the tornado and it may kill you. Just getting close to a tornado will subject you to dangerous flying objects that can injure or kill you.

What to do:

* Use the vehicle to immediately drive away from the storm if you have time.

* If the storm is too close get out of the car and lie in a ditch or other depression along the highway and away from any vehicles. If you cannot find any depressions close by and need to stay in your vehicle, tightly secure your seatbelt and keep below the windows. If you have any clothing in the car wrap up in it to protect your head and neck.

Remember in many tornadoes you will have very little time to decide what action you must take. Think about the proper action you should take before a storm hits. Choose carefully, since your life may depend on it. How to respond in this type of emergency should be well thought out and rehearsed with your family often.

Earthquakes

Earthquakes are one of the most destructive and frightening disasters on earth. An earthquake is the sudden shaking of the earth caused by the shifting of subterranean rocks or plates.

As these huge subterranean plates slowly move over time they pass over and under each other. At times they meet and lock up. The plates have no way to move to release the energy they build up. As this tremendous energy continues to build up it can suddenly break free causing the sudden shaking of the earth causing death and massive property damage.

Earthquakes are likely the most difficult disaster to prepare for because you do not know when or where they will strike. They happen suddenly and without any warning.

The damage from earthquakes is not just measured by a reading on a Richter Scale. Two earthquakes having the same magnitude may have very different destructive effects depending on where they are located within the earth. A shallow earthquake that has a smaller Richter Scale reading for example can potentially cause much more damage than a larger but much deeper earthquake. Shallow earthquakes cause more shaking at the surface of the earth and create more cracks in the earth's crust. These shallow earthquakes can cause more damage particularly if they are centered closer to where you live or work.

Alan Corson

What Steps Do I take?

The first step in earthquake preparation is to carefully assess where your home is built.

Homes built on sandy soil do not fare well in earthquakes. Homes built on solid rock fare much better. Even smaller earthquakes cause violent shaking that can force deep underground water to the surface mixing quickly with sandy soil turning it into almost liquid. Foundations hit by severe shaking and lateral movement cannot cope with this stress, and the home is torn apart. This same effect happens to commercial buildings, streets, freeways and factories.

The next step after evaluating the location of your home is to research the history of earthquakes in your area. You may believe that you are not at risk for earthquakes where you live but there are actually 45 states and territories throughout the United States that are identified as being at a moderate to high risk for earthquake activity. Many parts of the world are known to be high risk for earthquakes.

When asked, most people think the west coast of the United States is the only area in America where people should prepare for earthquake disaster. The media gives substantial coverage about the dangers of earthquakes particularly in California along the famed San Andreas Fault. Little media attention is given to other areas that also are at risk for earthquake disaster.

People living in areas not recently known for earthquake activity become complacent because there has not been an earthquake there for a long time. What they do not realize is they may be living in the same area that has produced massive earthquakes in the past. History has a tendency of repeating itself in these disasters.

People forget that in 1811-1812, New Madrid along the Mississippi River had the most powerful earthquake to hit the eastern United States in recorded history. This area is now within Missouri. That earthquake was felt 1,200 miles away and caused massive damage. This earthquake was so massive it changed the course of the Mississippi River for more than 100 miles!

Carefully research to see what the history of earthquakes is in your area. Plan accordingly.

Disaster Plan

The next step is to make a good disaster plan based on all of the information you have. The first part of your disaster plan is to insure that everyone in your family has a place to go in case you are not home and are separated when an earthquake hits. This is particularly important if your home is located in an area where it is likely to be severely damaged or destroyed in an earthquake. This meeting place should be a large open area such as a park, school play ground or large field.

Locate the closest emergency shelter such as the Red Cross or other emergency shelters in your area. Make sure all members of the family know of these locations in the event they need to go there after a disaster. If at home or work, plan your route to these shelters in case you cannot drive there.

As in any disaster you will have your home survival supplies including food, water and other items that have previously been listed. Make sure that these supplies are readily available to you in the event that you need to quickly evacuate after an earthquake.

It is always a good idea to keep your important papers in a waterproof container that is easy for you to grab if you need to quickly evacuate your home. It is also good to routinely electronically scan and back up all of your important financial records, files, insurance records and computer documents to an outside source where it is secure and protected in the event your home is destroyed by the earthquake or fire.

As in any disaster if you decide to evacuate be sure to leave a note at home that gives detailed information to rescue personnel of the date and time you left home, names of those with you, where you are going, when you expect to arrive at your destination, the manner of your transportation, the route you expect to take and emergency telephone numbers they can call.

If you want to understand how to prepare for an earthquake disaster just remember that the power grid will be out of service. Water lines will have been destroyed. Normal utilities will not be operating. There will be no telephone service and transportation will be difficult if not impossible. Stores will have their shelves stripped bare within hours and you will not be able to get any survival necessities after the disaster happens. Many of the roads and bridges in the disaster area will be damaged and impassible by motor vehicle. The normal supplies to the area by commercial trucks will end because of damaged roads and bridges. Prepare to be on your own for at least 10-15 days without any outside assistance. In a catastrophic earthquake you may not have restored services or food supplies for several months or longer. If you are not able or not prepared to survive on your own for that long then consider using your disaster evacuation plan and leave.

While you are thinking of your disaster preparation, think about the last television media coverage that you saw on an earthquake disaster. Remember watching the television and seeing not just a few but hundreds of people walking around dazed. They appeared to be in shock and stunned by the events that unfolded around them. They looked as if they had been exposed to a war zone. Homes were destroyed around them, fires were burning out of control, and people were injured and killed. Their world was turned completely upside down.

Many of these people may have put away some extra food and maybe some water in preparation for an earthquake. Many of them thought they were prepared. They were not.

When the disaster hit, the world as they knew it came to an end. They were seen wandering around helpless with no idea of what they were going to do. They had no idea of where they were going to go. They were waiting for someone to come to rescue them and to tell them what to do. They did not have the necessary preparation to deal with this disaster.

Sadly, even though these individuals put away some food and water they were completely unprepared for an earthquake. They did not have a disaster plan. They were not prepared.

This is the specific reason that you make a good disaster plan, discuss it often and practice it with your family so you will know what to do when a disaster strikes. You and every member of your family will have a good disaster plan, and alternate plans if needed so you will know what to do and where to go should a disaster happen.

Things around you will likely be more catastrophic than you have ever seen before in your life. Mentally prepare for that. Understand what happens in a major earthquake. Understand that these will be the conditions that you will face if that disaster happens. Knowing that, understanding that, and being prepared for that will be an enormous help if disaster ever strikes.

Many of us remember as children practicing fire drills at school. We performed these drills routinely. We knew what to do and where to go if a fire should happen. If a fire ever happened at school there is no doubt that we would have done exactly as we were trained to do even though we may have been frightened because of the smoke and fire. We knew what to do to survive. We had a "disaster plan." We were prepared. Remember, those people who train will always revert back to their training in a crisis. Those who do not train will almost always panic. Make a good disaster plan for your family. Practice it often.

During an Earthquake

* Find something heavy that you can get under for cover. A large desk or other piece of furniture will keep things from falling on you. If you are in bed roll off and remain beside the bed on the floor. The bed will absorb heavy objects that may fall protecting your position on the floor.

* DO NOT go outside during an earthquake. Falling objects, flying glass and other debris can be deadly during the

earthquake. This is particularly important if you live in the city.

If You Are Outdoors

* Move away from any buildings. Flying glass and falling debris can be deadly.

* Try to get into an open area away from any falling hazard.

* Keep away from any overhead power lines. Remain in a clear open area until the earthquake is over.

* If you are on the beach move to higher ground as soon as possible as earthquakes can cause deadly tsunamis. Don't wait until you can actually see a tsunami because the chances are you will not be able to move out of the area fast enough before the huge wave hits.

In a Moving Vehicle

* Slow down and try to drive to an area away from buildings, overpasses and power lines.

* Stop in a safe area and stay in your vehicle but not on freeway overpasses. Stop in an area that you will not likely be hit by other motorists. Turn on your lights and emergency flashers to make your car more visible to other motorists.

* After the earthquake proceed slowly looking for damage to the road, bridges and freeway overpasses.

After The Earthquake is Over

* Always be prepared for aftershocks which are quite common. Some of these aftershocks can be quite severe.

* Be alert to help anyone who has been injured or may have become trapped in the earthquake. Give medical aid as required. In heavily damaged buildings it is best to not rush in and try to dig a trapped person out on your own. You may dislodge fallen items that will cause you to become trapped as well. Let the person know that they have been found and immediately notify proper authorities who are equipped to rescue people in these circumstances.

* Do not enter damaged buildings. Broken glass and sharp objects make this a hazardous area after an earthquake. Minor aftershocks can make these areas especially deadly.

* Check your home for damage. Be sure to check to see if any electrical or gas service has been damaged in the earthquake. If you smell gas do not turn on any appliances. Leave the home immediately, notify authorities of the danger, and go somewhere safe.

If You Are Trapped

* Depending on where you are try to move as little as possible to avoid ingesting toxic dust from the rubble. Try to make enough room that you can breathe comfortably.

* If possible cover your mouth with a piece of cloth to protect you from breathing in toxic dust.

* Find something that you can use to tap on a pipe or other object to let rescue personnel know where you are. Rescue personnel will be actively searching for survivors so remain calm and organize your thoughts on how best to alert people to where you are. If you have a cell phone dial 911. Continue this even if the 911 lines are busy.

KNOTS

The ability to tie a good knot is an invaluable survival skill. There are literally hundreds of knots, some for very specialized purposes. If you are able to master the skill of tying only a few of these knots you will be much better prepared for any survival event. You can find many books that give an extensive list of various knots and how to tie them. Most people will not take the time to learn more than a few knots. The following are some good knots to learn. These are easy to learn, easy to tie and easy to untie to save the cordage.

Square Knot This knot is useful for joining shorter pieces of cordage together.

Clove Hitch Knot This type of knot ties a length of rope to an object. The knot is not as secure as some other knots but it works very well for certain applications when the line is under constant tension. This knot is also simple to tie.

Bowline Knot This is one of the most important knots to learn. This knot will not slip and will hold tight. An all purpose knot that will come in useful for any survival situation.

Figure Eight Knot A simple and effective knot to keep the end of a rope or cordage from coming out or undone.

Surgeon's Knot The Surgeon's Knot is an easy knot to tie and is used to join two lines of near equal size together.

Sheet Bend Knot A very effective knot used to join two ends together even if different sizes of cordage is used. It is a very simple knot to tie. It never slips and can be quickly untied.

Learn these knots both for camping, working around home and in the event you need to use them for your survival. Practice these knots often with a small length of cord or rope and you will find many uses for them.

Better yet, get several 3' lengths of small rope or cord and have members of the family practice tying these basic knots. Make this a fun activity for the whole family. See if family members are eventually able to tie these knots in the dark or without looking at the rope. These are important skills that will last a life time.

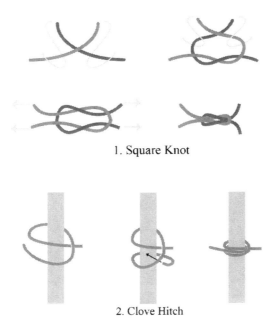

1. Square Knot

2. Clove Hitch

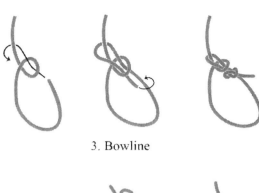

3. Bowline

4. Figure Eight Knot

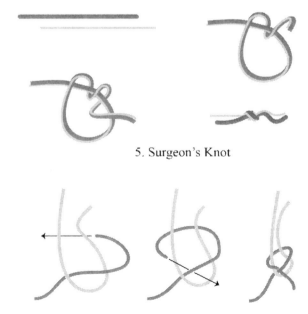

5. Surgeon's Knot

6. Sheet Bend

FIRST AID

Immunizations

The first step to insure you and your family are protected from health issues is to make sure that everyone in your family is current on all immunizations. Make this a priority for everyone in your family. Keep a current record of these immunizations at home.

Arrival At The Scene Of Injury

Whenever you respond to an emergency it is very important that you stop and assess the situation from a distance. Resist the temptation to rush in to help. By visually assessing the situation from a distance you have time to calm down and make good decisions.

You must insure your own safety before you can help others. It does no good to rush into a dangerous situation to help, only to find that you have stumbled into an area of poisonous fumes, toxic chemicals, downed live power lines or other calamity that makes you just one more victim that needs to be rescued.

Always assess the injuries to the victims at the scene before becoming involved. It may be difficult to do but in disasters with multiple victims you need to triage and bypass those who are so severely injured that they likely will not survive. It is a waste of time and supplies to spend time treating those critically injured who are likely to die rather than treat individuals who have serious life threatening injuries that could be saved.

First Aid Kit

Having a well stocked first aid kit could save your life, the lives of your family members, or others. It is not enough to simply have a first aid kit available, you must have the basic skills on how to use the first aid materials to properly treat an injured person. Parents along with everyone 12 years and older should take a basic first aid class. Practice these skills so you are ready to use them if necessary.

Millions of people are injured in or at home every year. These injuries are *not* the result of any disaster. These are everyday injuries that people sustain resulting in bruises, lacerations, scalding burns, broken bones, and other injuries. Add the ingredients of an earthquake, hurricane, tornado or flood and you will begin to see how important it is to have a good medical kit at home and the knowledge to use it.

When a disaster does occur you may not be able to use your telephone to get through to 911 for emergency help. You can expect 911 emergency circuits for police and fire to be overloaded and unavailable. You are on your own.

Even if you were fortunate enough to get through to 911, rescue personnel may not be able to reach your home. You too may not be able to travel from your home to reach medical assistance because of impossible roads, washed out bridges or flooding. Even if you were lucky enough to drive to a medical facility, medical personnel will quickly be overwhelmed with hundreds of incoming patients, many of whom will simply not receive medical treatment.

The fact is you will be faced with coping with these injuries yourself. Enroll in a basic CPR training class to learn basic life saving techniques. Ordinary injuries that occur in our normal daily lives can suddenly become life threatening events after a disaster.

You must take every precaution to prevent injuries particularly in a disaster. Falling objects in homes are frequently associated with personal injury. In many disasters you can avoid this danger by going to an area in your home that is free from these hazards.

With basic training and a good first-aid kit you will be able to properly treat many of the injuries that occur in your everyday life, and injuries that may occur in a disaster.

When putting together a good home first-aid kit, first assess who the kit may be used on. Are there children in the home, individuals with a known medical condition or elderly people who may need special medical treatment? If so, you may want to add other special items to the kit.

First, put together a basic medical kit including those critical items that you will need to treat the most common injuries. With that done you can begin adding those extra medical supplies that round out your kit.

Your medical kit should be stored in an area that is easy to get to. You don't want to pack this kit away "in case of an emergency" and then have to dig through three years of Christmas ornaments to find it.

Open Wounds

Open wounds are serious, not only because the victim has tissue damage and blood loss, but also because of the risk of infection. Infection becomes much more of a problem after a disaster when basic utilities are no longer available such as clean running tap water. In a contaminated disaster environment you risk infection from many elements such as contaminated water, air, soil and clothing. An open wound has a much higher risk of becoming infected after a disaster. If the wound becomes infected it will require more advanced treatment.

The medical kit should be put into a container that has several individual compartments to separate the type of medical equipment. This makes your first aid kit easier to use. You can use a fishing box or plastic tool kit or even a piece of luggage to store these items.

This home medical kit will be completely separate from the much smaller medical kit that you keep in your bug-out-bag. Since this is a home medical kit, you probably will not be lugging it around in the mountains and you can normally stock substantially more material in this kit for advanced medical treatment.

Home First-Aid Kit Supplies

* Sterile 4"x4" gauze—three packages or one for each member of the family

* Sterile 2"x2" gauze—three packages or one for each member of the family

* Gauze rolled bandages (4"-6" to secure dressings)

* Triangular bandage—two (can be made yourself in an emergency)

* Variety of band-aid type dressings (for small cuts and abrasions)

* Absorbent bandage dressings—(large and small)

* Bag of sterile cotton swabs

* Wire splint

* White medical tape (1-2 rolls)

* Trauma scissors

* Tweezers

* Adhesive cloth tape (2-3 rolls)

* Blister bandages

* Package of sewing needles (removing splinters, etc)

* Package of suturing needles and suturing thread
* Bottle of Hydrogen Peroxide
* Bottle of Rubbing Alcohol
* Antibiotic Ointment (1-2 tubes)
* Povidione Iodine—(2 bottles)
* Benadryl (or generic—topical for insect bites, etc)
* Neosporin cream (2 tubes)
* Aloe Vera Gel
* Calamine Lotion
* Glass thermometer (in protective case)
* Vinyl (latex-free) medical gloves (one box)
* Antiseptic gel
* Safety pins

Medications

* Aspirin / Tylenol / Ibuprofen
* Pepto Bismol
* Tums

Special Medical Equipment

If there is a person in your family that has a special medical condition such as diabetes you will need to include specialized medical items in your kit.

* Prescription Glucagon Injection

* Ketodiastic

* Insulin syringes and injectable insulin

* Sugar or juice treat for hypoglycemia

* Glucometer, lancet, strips—notebook & paper to record readings

It is important that you evaluate the specific needs for each family member and adjust your medical kit accordingly. For example, children's medication for pain may include acetaminophen (Tylenol) in the proper delivery such as droplets for small infants, chewable tablets for older children and ordinary tablets for adults.

Medical Assistance To Others

After a disaster people may come to you or ask for your help with an injured individual. Always be prepared to help others. Being properly trained for basic first aid and having a well stocked first aid kit will allow you to put your skills to work and help others in their time of need.

Medical Check—CPR:

* C-A-B: Compressions, Airway, Breathing (Not ABC's: Airway, Breathing and Compressions)

The American Heart Association has revealed new recommendations on the way to perform CPR. This new method substantially increased the oxygen-rich blood circulating through the victim's body during a medical emergency and increased the likelihood of them being revived at the scene.

Previously we were taught to perform the "ABC's" of CPR: Airway, Breathing and Compressions on a person who was down and not breathing. People were taught to first tilt the victim's head back to open the airway, then pinch the victim's nose and give a succession of breaths into the mouth and then lastly perform chest compressions.

Now the American Heart Association states that to initiate CPR you should first begin with chest compressions that will immediately push oxygen-rich blood through the victim's body. This is a vital first step for those who have had a heart attack. After chest compressions, then move on to make sure the airway is clear with the head tilted back and lastly perform the mouth to mouth successions of breaths. This medical change applies to all adults, children and infants but not for newborns.

There is the belief by some that transporting a victim to the hospital as quickly as possible substantially benefits that person's chance to recover and survive. Medical evidence indicates that this is not the case. If a person is down and is not resuscitated at that location, it is unlikely that they will benefit from any subsequent hospital treatment. These patients generally do not survive even after arriving at the hospital.

Here are the steps for the new CPR:

1. Shake and try to get the person to respond. If no response, roll the person onto their back.

2. Begin with chest compressions. Place the heel of your hand on the center of the person's chest. Spread your fingers and place your other hand on top of the first interlocking the fingers.

3. Begin compressions by pressing down at least 2" on the chest. Use your upper body and not just your arms to make these compressions. Lock your elbows. For children and infants, press down 1/2 of an inch. The compression rate should be about 100 times a minute, a bit faster will be okay. While performing compressions on a victim you may hear pops and snaps from the victim's chest. That is normal and you should not stop the CPR. Remember, there is very little that you can do to make the situation worse. If you stop the CPR the victim will likely die.

4. After the compressions, move on to open the airway by tilting the head back and lifting the chin up. Check the mouth for any obstructions that may have impaired the victim's ability to breath. You may use a mouth-to-mouth CPR barrier from your medical kit if you have one. This provides a barrier between your mouth and the mouth of the victim during rescue breathing.

5. Then close the victim's nose by pinching with your fingers. Take a normal breath, cover the victim's mouth with yours making a tight seal and then give two "one second breaths" and look to see if the victim's chest rises. That tells you that air is getting into the victim's lungs. Then resume compressions.

   After about two minutes of chest compressions and rescue breaths, stop and check the victim for breathing. If the victim is still not breathing you must continue CPR beginning with chest compressions. You should check for breathing about every two minutes or until medical assistance arrives. If the victim begins breathing or becomes conscious you can stop the CPR.

6. Continue CPR by giving 30 compressions, 2 breaths until the victim revives or more advanced medical help arrives. If you get tired have someone else continue this process. Continue CPR until the person is revived or until you are certain that continued CPR efforts will not be helpful.

Just Compressions—CPR

It is unfortunate but many people do not know how to give CPR or are reluctant to put their mouth on the mouth of someone who is not a member of their family. Others become stressed and excited in a traumatic event. They cannot remember how many breaths to give, how many compressions, and at what rate they should be given. They are afraid to do something that will aggravate the situation. In attempting to perform CPR to resuscitate a person there is very little that you can do to make the situation worse so always attempt to give CPR if you are ever faced with that situation.

It is important to understand that if immediate action is not taken the person will die. You must act quickly. Time is critical in these medical matters. If you are able to perform CPR, perform it with the new American Heart Association method of Compressions, Air and then Breathing.

The good news is that individuals who have suffered heart attacks have been found to benefit from just receiving the compression part of the CPR.

There have been studies in America that show that adults in many cases tend to survive cardiac arrest when just given continuous chest compressions that stimulate a heartbeat when compared to the traditional CPR method that uses mouth to mouth breathing.

If for any reason you cannot perform this full CPR technique then give the victim CPR by giving chest compressions only.

The human brain needs oxygen and begins dying soon after oxygen is cut off. You will not be able to wait for a few minutes for someone more trained to arrive to help. A few minutes means the difference between living and dying in these cases.

It is best to learn current CPR so you will be prepared in the event you need to use this skill to save a life. And remember, the vast majority of instances where CPR is needed happen at home. If you perform CPR in your lifetime, you will most likely perform it on someone that you love.

CPR On Infants

1. On infants more than two months old jostle the child and call out their name to get them to respond. You need to be aggressive in doing this but not to the point of hurting the infant. Try to wake them up.

2. If there is no response have someone call 911 and explain the circumstances. You should stay with the infant. If the infant is not breathing (put your head close to their mouth to make sure, listen for any breaths), put two fingers on the infant's breastbone directly between the nipples. Push straight down on the infant's chest about 1.5 inches. Immediately let up allowing the chest to rise completely. Repeat this process 30 times, which is about twice per second. If you have had CPR training to administer rescue breaths to infants then proceed and cover the entire mouth and nose of the baby with your mouth. Gently blow into the baby's mouth and nose until you see the chest rise. Let the air escape and the chest will go back down. Give one more gentle breath in the same manner. If no air is getting into the infant during rescue breaths, tilt the baby's head back and try again. You want a good open airway. Watch for the chest to rise when breaths are given. If you are unable to get air into the child for some reason, return to performing chest compressions at the same rate of twice per second. Try rescue breathing again after one set of compressions.

   It is important to understand that if you cannot determine if the baby is breathing but you find no signs that they are, assume that the baby is not breathing and proceed with infant CPR. It is much worse to assume the infant is breathing in these circumstances and do nothing at all.

Heimlich Maneuver

Choking due to an obstructed airway is a leading cause of accidental death. The Heimlich Maneuver is a simple emergency technique that can save a life. This technique will often dislodge food or another object that is caught in a person's airway causing them to choke. The maneuver increases the pressure in the abdomen and chest causing the object to be expelled. To perform the Heimlich Maneuver follow these steps:

1. Determine if the person is choking. You can see this behavior of a choking victim as they will have their hands around their throat and their facial appearances will be panicked. These individuals will not be able to speak and will have difficulty breathing since their airway is blocked. They will not be able to speak to you to tell you that they are choking. Left untreated the person will lose consciousness. This choking could result in their death.

2. Let the person know that you are going to help them. Have someone else call for emergency assistance but for now you must act to get the victim's airway open so they can breathe.

3. Stand the victim up if possible. The maneuver is easier to perform on a standing victim. If the person is too heavy for you or you are in a confined place you can perform the maneuver with the victim in a sitting position.

4. If the person is not able to breathe (you cannot hear any sound of air in and out) and the airway appears to be completely blocked, deliver several sharp blows with the heel of your hand to the area between the victim's shoulders to try to dislodge the item from their throat. If you are unsuccessful proceed with the Heimlich maneuver.

   Note, if the person is just having difficulty breathing and they are able to get some air in and out, do not use the back blows on that person as the partial obstruction may become lodged deeper completely cutting off the airway.

5. Get behind the person. Stand with your legs spread apart so that you have control of the victim in case they lose consciousness while you are holding them.

6. Reach around the victim with your hands around the victim's stomach. Make a fist with your dominate hand. Place your fist just above the victim's navel. Wrap your other hand around your fist.

7. Pull upward sharply pressing your fist into the victim's stomach with quick thrusts. Make these thrusts quick and forceful as if you are trying to lift the victim off of their feet. Perform 5-6 abdominal thrusts in quick succession. Repeat as necessary until the object is dislodged and spit out. When successful the victim will cough out the obstruction and will then be able to breathe.

   If the victim becomes unconscious during the procedure stop the thrust immediately. Check the mouth to see if you can see what is obstructing the airway and if it can be manually dislodged. If not, give the victim CPR until medical help arrives.

Lacerations

Small cuts are common but even small cuts have the risk of infection. To treat these injuries wash the area with soap and fresh water cleaning the wound area. Place topical disinfectant on the wound and then bandage.

Bleeding

Take immediate action to control injuries with severe bleeding. The most dangerous bleeding is arterial bleeding. Evidence of arterial bleeding is bright red blood that is pumping or pulsating from the body with the heartbeat. Venous blood is darker and is easier to control.

To treat bleeding, put direct pressure on the wound with a clean gauze pad. Make sure that the victim is lying down so that the wound area is elevated above the heart. This will help slow the bleeding. Place a bandage on the wound firmly but without cutting off circulation. After bleeding has been controlled, wash the wound carefully with a disinfectant and then apply a fresh clean bandage making sure that you do not cut off circulation.

Try to keep the person calm. If the victim remains excited the heart will only pump faster aggravating the situation.

Shock

Shock occurs at the slowing of the bodies normal functions, and may follow any injury regardless of how serious. Pain or cold will intensify shock. The symptom of shock includes weakness, anxiety, nausea, clammy skin with a weak and rapid heartbeat. The person may faint or lose consciousness. These symptoms occur because the victim's vital organs are not getting enough oxygen. Shock can become more critical than the initial injury itself and must be treated.

Keep the patient calm with their legs elevated in a position slightly higher than the person's heart. This will help the body circulate blood to vital organs.

In treating shock make sure the victim is breathing. Treat the injury to stop any bleeding. If fractures are present treat them.

Unless there is a head injury or a chest injury, put the patient on their back with their head and chest positioned lower than the legs. This position will help blood circulate to the brain and other vital organs.

If the victim has head or chest injuries, elevate the upper body to reduce bleeding.

If you are treating a person for shock and they become unconscious, turn the person over into a "face down" position with the head tilted to one side to keep the person from choking on their own blood or vomit. Make sure the person has a clear airway in that position. Keep the patient warm and continue monitoring the patient for any changes that may occur.

Bone Fractures

Bone fractures are basically of two types. The first is a (closed) fracture in which the bone remains closed within the skin. The second is the compound (open) fracture in which the bone has protruded through the skin.

In closed fractures there will be several symptoms:

1. The victim will have pain in the area of the fracture.

2. The victim may be unable to put any weight on the area of the fracture without experiencing pain.

3. You may hear the sound of bones grinding together at the site of the fracture during any movement of the area.

To treat a fracture, apply a splint that extends past the area above and below the fracture site. If the fracture appears likely to penetrate through the skin you may need to apply some traction to straighten the fracture deformity and then splint.

Put some type of padding in the splint for comfort and protection. Make sure that the splint does not cut off the circulation.

If you do not have a splint in your medical kit you can improvise and use a length of cardboard folded in thirds. Place some padding inside the cardboard and place around the area to be splinted. Secure the splint with tape, cloth or other cordage to secure it. In wilderness survival situations splint the injury with sticks on each side. Pad the splint with clothing. Secure the splint with strips of cloth or other cordage.

Sprains

Mild to moderate sprains can be treated at home with a basic first-aid kit. The first goal is to reduce the swelling and pain.

To treat a severe sprain, splint the area so that it is immobile. Leave the splint on until the pain is completely gone.

Use ice for the first 48 hours to reduce swelling and pain. Place ice in a wet towel or plastic bag covered with cloth. Apply on the injured area for 15 minutes every 2-3 hours. Do not leave the ice on while sleeping. Do not allow the ice to have direct contact with the skin as it could cause a cold burn to skin tissue. Keep the injured area elevated to help reduce swelling. Restrict physical activity until healed.

Heat Exhaustion

Heat exhaustion is a heat related illness that can occur after exposure to high temperatures and the body becomes dehydrated.

Symptoms of heat exhaustion are excessive thirst, headache, dizziness, fatigue, weakness, confusion, and loss of consciousness.

Without proper treatment heat exhaustion may progress into the more serious condition of heat stroke. Heat stroke can cause brain damage and death.

Heat exhaustion is not uncommon when the body has insufficient water. The body becomes dehydrated and salt-depleted.

Treatment

1. Get the person out of the heat and into an air conditioned room. If an air conditioned room is not available put them into a cool shaded area. Fan the person to cool them down. It is important to reduce the victim's body temperature as soon as possible.

2. If possible have the person take a cool shower or bath. Even a cool sponge bath will help cool them down.

3. Put wet towels on the person to cool their body or spray them with a garden hose to wet their clothing and cool them down.

4. Have the person drink plenty of cool water. Avoid coffee and alcoholic beverages.

5. Have them avoid physical activity for a day or so.

Individuals who are older than 65 and children up to age 5 are particularly vulnerable to heat exhaustion because their bodies adjust more slowly to heat conditions than others. This also applies to individuals taking some medications.

Individuals with health conditions such as heart problems, diabetes, obesity or those underweight can be at added risk for heat exhaustion.

Muscle Cramps

Muscle cramps occur when the muscles in the body accumulate excess lactic acid from the loss of too much salt through perspiration.

To treat muscle cramps have the victim rest and slowly stretch the aching muscles. Introduce small amounts of salt to regain proper salt balance.

Burns

Even small burns are serious and must be properly treated to avoid infection. Some superficial burns only affect the top layer of skin. More severe burns however, affect deep skin tissue. Any surface burn that is larger than about 6" needs advanced medical treatment.

Small Burns

For small burns remove any jewelry in case of swelling. Apply sterile gauze pads lightly coated with Aloe Vera, Vaseline or other suitable ointment and bandage the area lightly. Have the victim drink more water than normal.

Larger Burns

In larger burns you may notice body fluid weeping from the burn site. In these burns the victim faces the danger of shock. Put the victim down in a comfortable safe area. Remove any jewelry in the area of the burn in case of swelling. Cool the injury to prevent further damage. Remove any clothing that may come in contact with the skin to prevent infection. Lightly cover the burned area with a clean dressing. Get medical treatment as soon as possible.

Snow Blindness

Snow blindness is a condition that occurs when a person's eyes are exposed to excessive amounts of ultraviolet ray (UV Ray) without the protection of sunglasses. This condition is caused by the glaring reflection of the bright sunshine on either ice or snow. This bright light into the eyes causes the cornea of the eye to burn much like skin sunburn.

Like normal sunburns the effect is not generally felt until hours after the exposure.

Symptoms A person who has snow blindness may feel scratchy or burning sensations in the eyes. The eyes may tear excessively and appear bloodshot. The person may see a halo of light and experience temporary loss of vision. In more severe cases the eyes will feel like sand is in the eyes, and the eyes can swell completely closed. The corneas will normally heal in about 12 to 48 hours. Snow blindness is painful but it rarely results in permanent eye damage.

Prevention Snow blindness can be prevented by wearing a pair of good sunglasses or goggles that wrap around and cover the whole eye from the side or the edge of the eye to the nose. Sunglasses or goggles that offer a high UV ray protection are best. These glasses or goggles have darker lenses and greater visible light filtration.

Improvise—Make Your Own

You can improvise and make an adequate pair of snow glasses by taking a thin piece of cardboard, duct tape, magazine covers or other suitable material and making two thin, horizontal slits to see through. Add string to the ends to make the goggles. The small horizontal slits limit the amount of light coming into the eye.

Treating Snow Blindness

1. Remove any contact lenses that you may be wearing.

2. Do not rub your eyes even when they feel itchy.

3. Apply wet cool towels on the face to ease the pain and burning sensation. Take pain medication as required.

4. Cover both eyes with a soft wet cloth to protect them from light and further irritation.

Blisters

Blisters are small areas where the skin has pulled away and filled with fluid. Blisters are common on the feet when the skin has repeatedly been rubbed by shoes or boots.

Blood Blisters are those areas which appear red from skin damage that involves a blood vessel bleeding into the skin tissue. Blood blisters tend to occur more from a sudden traumatic impact or pinching of the skin rather than from repetitive friction of the skin tissue.

Prevention To prevent blisters make sure that your footwear fits properly. If you begin to feel an area on your feet that is getting chaffed, place a thin bandage or adhesive tape on that area to serve as a "second skin" to protect the area. Keep your feet as dry as possible. Wet footwear will cause a blister faster than dry footwear. Change your socks often and use a foot powder to help keep your feet dry.

You may need to pierce the blister to reduce the buildup of fluid and to reduce the associated pain. First wash the area well. Sterilize a needle by holding the end over a flame for a few seconds or wipe with rubbing alcohol. After the needle is cool pierce the edge of the blister allowing the fluid to drain. This is generally painless. Put pressure on the blister to drain all the fluid out. Apply a disinfectant and then bandage.

Bee Stings

Bee stings are common, painful but usually harmless unless you are allergic. Remove the stinger by using tweezers to gently pull the stinger to remove it. You can also use your fingernail to gently get the stinger out. Do not squeeze the venom sack. Remove the stinger as soon as possible to prevent more venom from being pumped into the skin.

Wasps, yellow jackets and hornets differ from honey bees in that they have stingers without barbs. These stingers are normally withdrawn after each sting. These insects are capable of stinging a victim several times (whereas the honey bee will sting one time leaving the barbed stinger in the victim's skin).

The normal reaction to a bee sting is redness and swelling in the area of the sting. Pain will usually subside in a couple of hours.

Some people are allergic to bee stings. This can cause a serious medical problem. Bee stings that cause an allergic reaction may cause the victim to develop swelling and hives on areas of the body away from where the sting occurred.

Allergic Reaction to bee stings include:

1. Nausea

2. Vomiting

3. Dizziness

In cases of anaphylactic reactions the victim will experience difficulty breathing. They can have a drop in blood pressure that may lead to shock if not treated. People who have allergic reactions to bee stings can expect any subsequent bee stings to have a worsened reaction. These individuals should have epinephrine available that can be injected to counter the bee sting.

Treatment

1. Apply ice to the area. The coldness from the ice constricts the blood vessels and slows the flow of venom. The ice will also numb the area and reduce pain and itching.

2. Wash the area with cold water and apply hydrocortisone cream to the sting site.

   If you do not have hydrocortisone you can improvise and make a tablespoon of paste from unseasoned meat tenderizer and fresh water. Spread the paste on the sting site. Meat tenderizer contains an enzyme called "papain" which can break down the toxins in the bee venom.

   Some relief can be experienced by mixing a paste of baking soda and water and applying that to the sting area.

3. Taking an antihistamine (Benadryl) can provide some relief from the pain.

   Any bee sting in the mouth, throat or nose is a serious incident even if the person is not allergic to bee venom. These stings can cause swelling that can impair the victim's ability to breath.

Mammal Bites

When a person is bitten by another human or animal it can cause tissue damage and infection. Proper first aid can help reduce the incidents of infection. This can also reduce scarring.

Treatment

Allow the wound to bleed for a few minutes as this will flush bacteria from the wound. If the wound is a laceration, apply pressure to stop excess bleeding.

1. Clean the wound immediately after the bite to help prevent infection.

2. Wash the wound with anti-bacterial soap. Continue washing the wound for several minutes to allow the soap to kill the germs. Then wash the area for several minutes allowing the fresh water to flush out bacteria.

3. Dry the area with a sterile pad or paper towel. Do not use ordinary towels as they tend to retain bacteria that can then be transferred to the wound.

4. Disinfect the wound by pouring Betadine or other disinfectants directly into the wound. If you do not have Betadine available, use hydrogen peroxide to flush and disinfect the wound.

5. Allow the wound area to dry out without blowing on the area as this will contaminate the wound area again.

6. Cover the wound with a sterile bandage. If swelling is present apply ice compacts.

7. Take Ibuprofen to help limit swelling.

Butterfly Bandages

Lacerations frequently occur and they come in a variety of sizes. The size and depth of these wounds will determine how they need to be treated. Many of these cuts can be treated with a butterfly bandage that holds the wound together until it can heal.

1. Clean the wound with hydrogen peroxide and anti-bacterial soap.

2. Allow to completely dry.

3. Attach the butterfly bandage on one side of the wound. If the wound is larger and you need more bandages, place two or three bandages on one side. Gently pull the butterfly bandages over the wound to the opposite side closing the wound evenly. Cover the butterfly bandages loosely with a topical bandage to keep the wound area clean.

Superglue

Superglue can be used to close a minor wound. The best superglue to use is the tube of anti-fungal super glue but any ordinary superglue will work. Try to use the type of superglue that is not runny since it is more difficult to work with and takes longer to dry. After you use a tube of superglue to treat a wound make sure to keep it out of your first-aid kit so it is not used again. Always use a fresh unopened tube for any subsequent wound. Do not risk infection with an old open tube.

1. Wash your hands well and then put on medical gloves. This will help in case you spill some superglue on your fingers. Set out some gauze pads to absorb any blood from the wound.

2. Clean the wound thoroughly with hydrogen peroxide and anti-bacterial soap. It is very important to clean and disinfect the wound properly. Take your time and do a thorough job with this. It may take 4-5 minutes to disinfect the wound properly.

3. Pinch the skin to line up both sides of the wound. See if the wound is such that the skin will realign when held together. If the skin will not align, you may not be able to superglue the wound and it may require stitches.

4. Align both sides of the wound. Dab the wound with a gauze pad to keep the area dry.

5. Apply the superglue starting at the highest area of the wound and move down without spilling onto the sides. Carefully apply the superglue in this manner. For head wounds, do not cut any hair away from the wound since it will push the superglue away when it grows back. Just hold the hair flat to the skin as you apply the superglue to the wound.

6. Hold the wound together and wait for the superglue to dry. Allow to dry thoroughly before releasing. Do not bandage the wound after the application of the superglue. Allow the wound to heal. Protect the wound from getting wet.

7. After 10 days or so you can apply Vaseline jelly or another petroleum product which will help break down the superglue over time.

In some cases the skin of the laceration will not line up or is too deep to superglue. In these cases you may need to suture the wound.

Suturing A Wound

When faced with a wound that is too deep for a bandage suturing may be required. The main purpose of any wound treatment is to protect the wound from infection, encourage the body's own healing process and insuring a good cosmetic result. God made the human body with amazing healing qualities.

Most injuries that occur do not require complex suturing techniques. If the wound is too severe and penetrates deep into the skin, or muscle then advanced medical help must be obtained.

If at all possible other wound closure methods should be given consideration before deciding on sutures.

If the decision is made to suture, the appropriate size suture thread of 4-0 is good for most lacerations and 3-0 for larger or deeper wounds. 5-0 is better for facial lacerations or when suturing tender skin.

If you are in a situation where there are no medical services available or out in the wilderness miles away from civilization, you may find it necessary to suture a wound on your own. Suturing a wound in field conditions has the risk of infection and careful consideration should be made as to whether it is best to leave the wound unsutured and allow it to heal on its own and possibly scar or to suture the wound.

If you find it necessary to suture the wound you need to perform the initial first aid and stop the bleeding. Then prepare to suture the wound if bleeding continues or if the wound is too deep to heal on its own.

1. Put on surgical gloves to help prevent infection.

2. Sterilize the wound area. Use anti-bacterial soap and clean the area well for several minutes. Wash with clean water for several minutes to clean and disinfect the wound.

3. Use the smallest needle and appropriate suture thread. You may need to improvise to use an unused barbless fishing hook that has been properly sterilized. Be sure no barbs are on the hook. If the fishing hook does have barbs file or flatten the barb before using. Use suture thread, sewing thread, unused fishing line or other suitable suture material. Make sure these items are also properly sanitized.

4. Pinch and hold the laceration edges together aligning them. Insert the needle through one side of the wound and then the other side of the wound at equal distances. The suture is taken only through the skin and not deeper into the underlying fat or muscle.

5. Pull the suture thread tight enough to pull both sides of the laceration together. Tie a knot in the suture thread putting the knot on one side of the wound and not on top. Suture spaces are normally about ¼" apart. When suturing the wound it may bleed. Dab a sterile gauze pad on the wound to remove the blood so the suturing can be finished. Leave about ¼" of suture thread above the wound so it can be accessed later when it is time to remove the suture.

6. Keep the wound clean. Monitor the wound during the next day or so for any signs of infection. In some cases it may be necessary to remove a stitch or two to allow the wound to drain.

If you have a small needle nosed pliers in your kit you can hold the needle or fishing hook to allow for sterilization with an open flame. This tool can also help you suture the wound since it will hold the needle or hook tight and will keep your fingers from becoming slick from the blood.

If the decision is made to suture a wound you need to do this as soon as possible. Wounds should be sutured no later than 6 hours from the time of injury. If you cannot suture by that time you may want to just leave the wound open and allow it to heal on its own.

After suturing a wound the sutures need to be removed in a timely manner. Sutures to the face need to be removed in about 5 days. Sutures on wounds to the limbs and trunk should be removed in 7-8 days. If you have sutured a wound over a joint where movement is common, that suture may need to remain for a few days longer.

Removing A Fish Hook

Getting impaled by a fish hook is a common occurrence. To remove the hook first cut any fishing line that is still attached to the hook. If the barb of the hook has passed through the skin to where it can be seen, cut the barb off or flatten it against the hook with pliers. You may also be able to snip off that portion of the hook with pliers. If the barb is just under the skin you may need to quickly push the hook through the skin so the barb penetrates the skin and is exposed. This is better than trying to pull the barbed hook back through the skin to get the hook out. Then cut the barb or flatten it against the hook shaft.

After the barb has been removed or flattened take a length of string and lay the string on the skin under the hook where it enters the skin. Pull the string while holding down on the shaft of the hook making it easier to remove the hook.

After removing the hook clean the injury with disinfectant and bandage it.

Tick Bites

Ticks are a parasite that can be found anywhere from remote wilderness areas to urban gardens. They are most active during the warmer months of the year. Ticks prefer moist areas and thrive in long grasses, in brush and under leaves. Ticks live by feeding on blood.

Most tick bites do not cause a serious health problem but some can carry diseases such as Lyme disease. It is best to remove a tick as soon as possible. It is important to remove the tick's head which at times can be difficult to see since some are very small.

To remove a tick, take a pair of tweezers and carefully grab the tick as close to its mouth (part stuck into your skin) as possible. Do not grab the tick around its middle since you may push infected fluids from the tick into your skin which will likely cause an infection. Gently pull up on the tweezers straight out until the tick's mouth lets go of your skin. This may take a few seconds for the tick to release its hold on your skin. Be sure that you do not twist the tick as this may break off the tick's head and leave it in your skin.

If you do not have tweezers put on medical gloves and then use your fingernail to gently lift the tick up and out of your skin. You can improvise and use the blade of a small knife to accomplish this too. Be sure that you do not cut the tick but simply use the blade to lift the tick up and out of your skin.

Things *not* to do:

1. Do not try to smother the tick using gasoline, rubbing alcohol, petroleum jelly or other such items. This may lead to infection when the tick regurgitates its fluids into your skin.

2. Do not try to burn the tick to force it out of your skin for the same reason.

Poison Ivy—Poison Oak—Poison Sumac

Poison Ivy, poison oak and poison sumac are plants that have oils that can cause an irritating rash when they come into contract with your skin. This oil is present in all parts of the plant including the leaves, stems, flowers, berries and roots. You can contract this oil even when touching the clothing, pets, equipment or other objects that have come into contact with these plants.

Common symptoms are:

1. Itchy skin where the plant came into contact with your skin

2. Red lines or steaks of redness where the plant touched your skin

3. Blisters filled with fluid that may seep out

Symptoms from these poisonous plants usually appear within 5-48 hours from initial contact with the plant. It is possible that you can get a reaction after several days. With each subsequent exposure to these poisonous plants you will find that the reaction time becomes much shorter.

The rash from these poisonous plants is not contagious. Another person cannot get this rash from the fluid watery blisters that may leak. The rash may appear to spread but that is because the person is likely developing other areas from earlier contact with the plant on different parts of the body.

Serious Symptoms:

Some people are particularly sensitive to the oil from these plants. They may develop:

1. Substantial swelling in the face, neck, genitals, and eye lids

2. Large blisters that form and leak out fluid.

How to Identify Poison Ivy

Poison Ivy has three pointed leaves that change color during the seasons. These leaves are reddish in the spring time and they turn green in the summer. In the fall these leaves turn to a yellow or orange-red color. This plant grows as either a vine or as a bush. The berries on poison ivy sometimes are white and that can help you identify this plant.

How to Identify Poison Oak

Poison oak also has three leaves that resemble the leaves of an oak tree. These plants grow in low shrubs and have long vines.

How to Identify Poison Sumac

Poison sumac has leaves that grow in groups of 7-13 leaves along the length of the plant stem. This plant can grow either as a tree or a shrub. The small yellowish flowers will grow into gloss white or off white berries.

Treatment

On occasion there may be times when you were just not able to avoid contact with one or more of these poisonous plants. Treatment after exposure includes:

1. Remove your clothes and place them into a bag where they will not contaminate other people or other clothing.

2. Take a shower as quickly as possible and wash your skin thoroughly with cool water and a mild soap that does not contain any oils. Quickly washing the plant's poisonous oils off your skin will help prevent most allergic reactions.

   If you are in the wilderness you can wash off in a lake or stream to remove the oils from your skin. Your clothes need to be washed thoroughly or you risk re-exposing your skin to these oils.

3. Apply cold compresses to relieve itching. Also try topical lotions or creams such as calamine lotion. Take antihistamine or other over the counter medicine. In a pinch you can make a paste out of three parts of baking soda to one part water. Apply the paste to the rash.

4. Avoid scratching these areas.

The best treatment for any of these plants is to be able to identify them and avoid them.

Car Emergency Kit

Think of all the time that you spend in your vehicle away from home. There are many occasions in which you travel from home and may encounter circumstances that leave you stranded. Basic emergency supplies should be kept in each of your vehicles.

1. Snow chains—tow rope or strap

2. Flares or reflective triangles

3. Jumper cables for battery

4. Gloves and throw tarp or sheet of heavy plastic to kneel on when changing tire

5. Spare tire, jack and tools

6. Bottled water and non-perishable foods

7. Basic first aid kit

8. Extra warm clothes, gloves and boots

9. Fire starting kit (matches, fire steel, candles, tinder)

10. Flash light and extra batteries (leave batteries out of flashlight to keep them fresh until needed)

11. Emergency blanket

12. Large knife or hatchet

13. Cordage

Alan Corson

How To Avoid Lightening

It is important to understand that there is no place safe outdoors when a thunderstorm is close. If you are close enough to hear thunder from the storm you are in range to be hit by lightening. This is true even if you are many miles away from the storm.

The best way to avoid a lightning strike is to find a closed shelter and remain there until the danger has passed. When inside a shelter stay away from anything electrical such as telephones, computers, and all other electrical appliances that could put you in direct contact with electricity. Stay away from plumbing since lightening can follow plumbing and wiring in the home. Keep away from windows as well.

If you are near a hard top vehicle get inside. Close the doors and roll up all windows. If lightening should strike the vehicle you will have some protection with the metal frame of the vehicle. The electricity will travel through the vehicle and to the ground. Do not use electronic equipment in the vehicle during the storm and keep your body away from the sides of the vehicle during the storm.

This is not the case with open topped cars, convertibles, ATV's or motorcycles as these do not offer any real protection from lightning strikes.

If you are outdoors and caught in a thunder and lightning storm here are the steps you need to take:

1. Quickly move away from any tall or isolated object. Do not use a tree as shelter. Look for any shelter that is out of the wind and is a good area that would avoid a lightning

strike. A depression or area between large rocks may serve as temporary shelter until the danger passes.

2. Lightning strikes to moving objects are much rarer than to stationary objects. If you are moving from one shelter to a better shelter run and do not stop until you reach your destination.

3. At times before lightening strikes if there is a sensation in which you feel your hair standing on end and a tingling sensation along your neck and arms you are in immediate danger of being hit by lightening. You need to turn and run as fast as you can. If you cannot run then crouch down on the balls of your feet with your feet close together. Tuck your chin into your chest. Do not lie down on the ground.

Pants As A Flotation Device

If you are ever in the situation where you are suddenly plunged into deep water with only your clothes on you can use your clothing to make an effective flotation device. You may be in a lake far from shore or in the ocean when you suddenly find yourself in the water with nothing else around you. You can tread water for only so long and then fatigue will set in and your survival chances are significantly reduced. Here is what you need to do to survive:

1. Remain calm. You need to think about what you are doing to make a flotation device that will save your life. Don't panic.

2. Remove your pants. You may need to take your boots or shoes off to do this. If possible tie the laces together and wrap them around your neck. You will need these when you make it to shore.

    Your pants will want to cling to your body but strip them off one leg at a time. You may go under water a bit while doing this but don't panic your pants will come off.

3. When your pants are off tie both pant legs together near the ankle area. This is done by simply crossing the pant legs and tying them together as low on the pant leg as possible. Make this knot as tight as you can. Zip up or button the pants.

4. Grab the waist area of the pants lifting them into the air and shake the pants to fill the pant legs with air. Quickly lower the waist of the pants into the water below the surface so the air in the pant legs is trapped making the pant legs buoyant.

5. Hold the waist of the pants under water and slip your head in between the two pant legs. Put your arms over the top of the pant legs. The waist of the pants is at your front. You now have a flotation device.

6. Now use one hand to hold open the waist of the pants while you use your other hand to rapidly splash water and lots of air bubbles into the waist of the pants. Do this for 10-15 seconds. Then push the waist area under water when you have filled the pants with air. The oxygen filled water will be trapped inside the pant legs and will keep the pants afloat. As time passes the air will slowly escape

so you just repeat the process to refill the pants with air. You can use this technique to keep you afloat for hours or even days.

You should practice this technique in a swimming pool, lake or other suitable location. Learn how to perform this life saving technique.

Personal Hygiene

Personal Hygiene is often overlooked when preparing for a disaster. Personal hygiene is an important part of keeping healthy. There are several things that must be considered for survival hygiene:

1. Wash your hands often. This seems simple but after a disaster or when you are in the wilderness it is very easy to focus your attention on other matters and neglect this important hygiene issue. This is especially important when preparing food and handling cooking utensils. Washing your hands is a very good way to avoid parasites and harmful pathogens that may compromise your ability to survive.

2. Bathe. You can improvise and make a suitable bath by using your tarp, sheet of plastic or even a cut out garbage bag. Place the material in a shallow depression in the ground or on flat ground just build up the sides with sticks, soil or other material to create a basin. Use surface water with a bit of heated water from a fire to create a nice warm bath. Having a medium size hand towel and wash cloth makes bathing easier and you will use much less water.

To improvise a wilderness shower take an empty container such as a coffee can and punch several small holes in the bottom. Punch two holes near the lip and insert a wire or cord that allows you to hang the tin in a tree. Pour warm water from the campfire into the tin and allow the water to slowly sprinkle out of the tin onto your skin. Get wet, soap up, and then rinse off. Add water to the tin as needed.

In extremely cold conditions when outside bathing is not practical, you can warm just a quart or two of water to bathe. Use a bit of water to get wet, soap up, and then rinse off with the rest of the water. With experience you will be able to bath with just one quart of water.

3. Wash Your Clothing. Washing your clothing is important since extended wear will hold dead skin and can harbor diseases ready to infect any small scratch or cut you may get. You can wash your clothes in available water sources and hang them out to dry. Freshly washed clothing is much easier on the smell as well.

    If water is in short supply you can shake out your clothes and then put them in direct sunlight, since we know the sun's ultraviolet radiation and fresh air can kill certain bacteria and pathogens. Be sure to expose all of the cloth to direct sunlight for several hours to get the best benefit of the sun's cleaning.

4. Keep your hair clean

5. Keep your teeth clean—remember to never use contaminated surface water to brush your teeth.

6. Keep your feet clean and dry. Change your socks if your feet ever get wet. Air out your boots to keep them dry. In wet climates put your boots on sticks set upside down near the fire to dry out. Be sure that you do not put the boots too close that they catch on fire.

7. Sanitation. It is important to dispose of human waste properly. At home when you do not have running water or toilets available you can use a five gallon bucket with short pieces of plywood or 2x4's on the sides as the seat. Put the lid on after each use to keep the flies out and smell under control. When close to full you will need to carry the waste a good distance away from your home and bury it or burn it. Do not allow these wastes to be anywhere near where you are living, cooking or eating.

If you are in the wilderness and in a stationary location for a period of time designate a toilet area at least 200 feet from your camp. Make sure this area is not near your water source and is downhill from your camp. You may need to dig a trench or pit for toilet activities. You can put small logs or large sticks across the trench or pit to allow you to sit while using this make shift toilet. It is always a good idea to throw a layer of soil over recent use to help keep flies out and reduce the smell.

Survival is not about personal toughness but instead is about mastering some very important skills to learn what to do in a survival situation. These skills are not difficult and many older children are able to master them with practice.

To save your life and the lives of those you love, it is very important that you practice all of these survival skills before you actually need them. When faced with a disaster and your life and the lives of your family are at stake, you will be scared and concerned about survival. That is definitely not the time to begin learning survival skills and how to stay alive. Survival skills require time and dedication to the practice. Hopefully, you will never be faced with a life and death survival situation . . . but if you ever are, and you have practiced the skills described in this book you will have the confidence knowing that you <u>will</u> be able to survive.

You may want to keep this survival book in your bug out bag for reference. Good Luck!

CPSIA information can be obtained
at www.ICGtesting.com
Printed in the USA
FSOW01n2212180316
18187FS